Table of Contents

MARTIN COUNTY
Community Redevelopment Agency

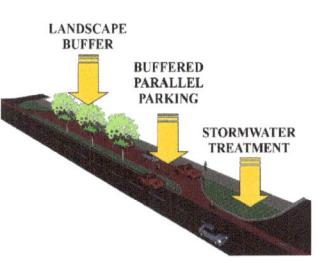

Executive Summary

CRA Successes

The Martin County Community Redevelopment Agency's (CRA) seven redevelopment areas undertook many planning projects and coordinated private development projects in fiscal year 2014. These projects which are detailed within this annual report where conceived by the residents of the redevelopment area and adopted in the seven community redevelopment area Community Development Plans.

The CRA saw renewed interest from the private sector to invest in the redevelopment areas. In 2014, the CRA saw an increased in the number of development inquiries and building permits issues. In 2014, there was a $1.4 million dollar increase in permit valuations by the private sector within the redevelopment areas compared to the previous year. These investments are leading to a growth in the County's tax base and a growth in the Tax Increment Finance (TIF) revenue for the CRA.

Project Highlights

The 12-month period ending September 30, 2014 included various highlights throughout the Martin County Community Redevelopment Agency's seven Neighborhood Planning Areas:

CRA WIDE PROJECTS

The Community Redevelopment Agency (CRA) spearheaded several initiatives designed to benefit all seven community redevelopment areas as a whole:

- Provided Redevelopment Technical Assistance for properties within the redevelopment areas.
- Conducted design review and permitting for projects throughout the Planning Areas.
- Coordinated with Martin County Departments for possible acquisition of blighted properties in the CRA.
- Continued to draft the Community Oriented Code which will streamlined the code for redevelopment.

GOLDEN GATE

- Completed Golden Gate Neighborhood Stormwater Retrofit Study.
- Acquired vandalized, fire damaged property cited for multiple ongoing code violations for redevelopment.

HOBE SOUND

- Conceptual design for the Bridge Road main street completed. Final Engineering and right of way donations underway.
- Proposed the creation of a Micro Action Plan for the Banner Lake Neighborhood

INDIANTOWN

- Village Square II received site plan approval and announced Dunkin Donuts as the primary tenant.
- Carter Park nationally recognized as a model public private partnership.

JENSEN BEACH

- Continued design and planning activities for Indian River Drive "Complete Streets" transformation.
- Design for the Jensen Beach Connector project started.

OLD PALM CITY

- Continued design and planning for the Mapp Road Town Center streetscape improvement project to include innovative stormwater management.
- Initiated design for the Charlie Leighton Park Accessible Floating Dock.
- Completed installation of a demonstration rain garden on Mapp Road.

PORT SALERNO

- Completed Commerce Ave. Demonstration Project
- Started design for the Manatee Creek Micro Area Action Plan (MAP) Phase I Project.
- Started design for the Salerno Road Sewer Enhancement Project

RIO

- The Rio Porches development received all permits and is under construction. Water and sewer were extended south on Orange Avenue.
- Completed design of the Rio Community Message Sign.
- Completed installation of landscape improvements on western CR-707.

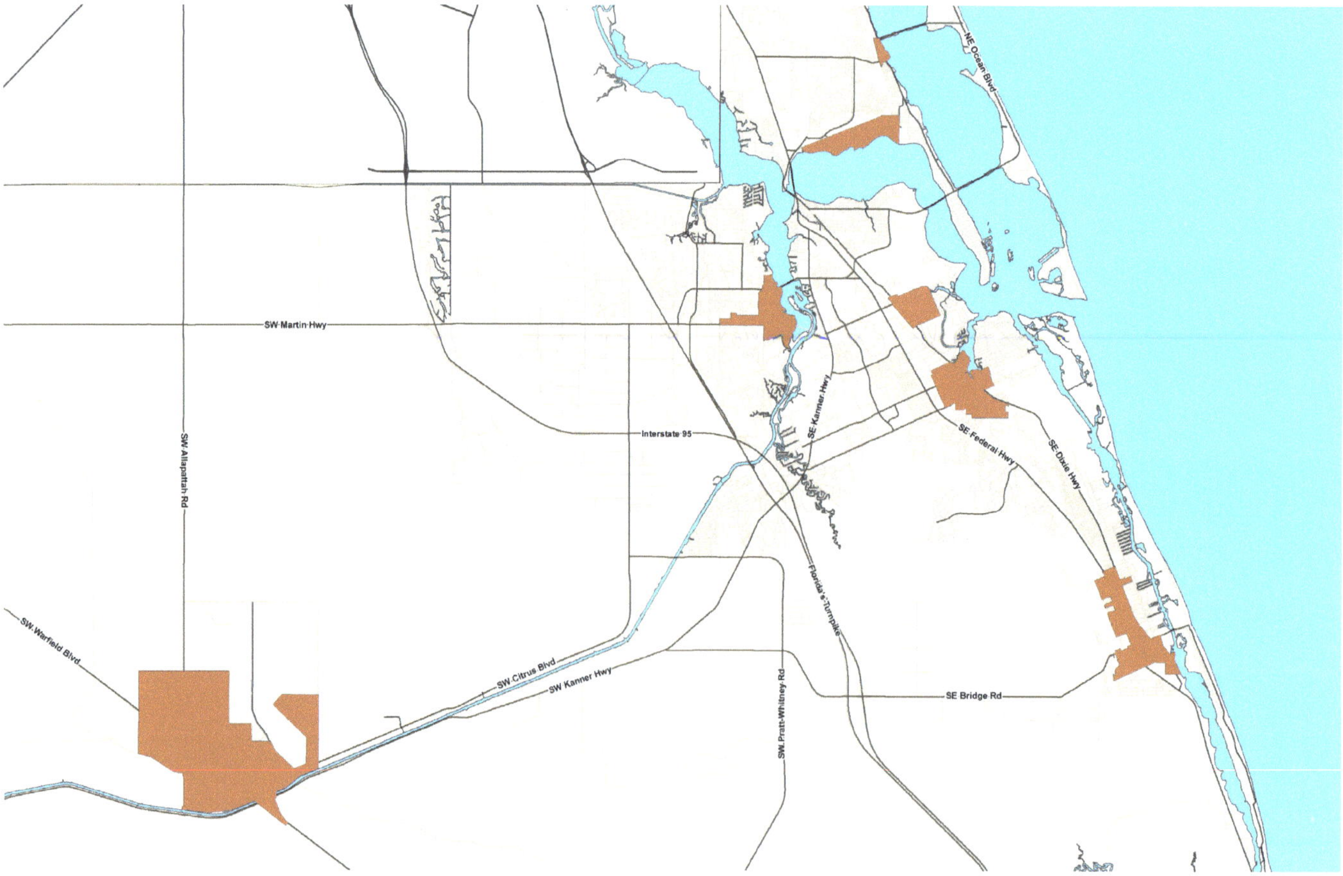

MARTIN COUNTY
Community Redevelopment Agency

Introduction

The Martin County Community Redevelopment Agency (CRA) is pleased to submit the Annual Report for fiscal year ending September 30, 2014, as required by Florida Statute Section 163.356(3)(c) and Martin County Code Section 39.3.B.5.

It is the philosophy of the Community Redevelopment Agency to keep all interested parties informed with respect to the activities of the CRA and to encourage active participation in the implementation of redevelopment programs benefiting the entire community. This report enables readers to gain an understanding of CRA's operation and financial activity for fiscal year 2014.

This annual report outlines the activities and programs that the Martin County Community Redevelopment Agency managed, funded, collaborated, or supported, between October 1, 2013 and September 30, 2014. This Report also reflects cooperation and coordination in planning, redevelopment, and development activities between and among the Martin County CRA, County Departments, citizens, regional agencies, and state and federal government agencies.

We believe the data, as presented, is accurate in all material respects and that all necessary disclosures have been acknowledged.

What is a CRA?

A Community Redevelopment Agency (CRA) is a public entity that finances redevelopment within focused areas. These areas tend to be older neighborhoods where there is a need to reverse deterioration, create jobs, revitalize the business climate, increase property values and encourage active participation and investment by citizens.

In order to be legally established, a Community Redevelopment Agency (CRA) must adhere to the guidelines as outlined in the Community Redevelopment Act (Chapter 163, Part III, Florida Statutes). In summary, the Act outlines the process for creating a CRA as follows:

1. Adopt the Finding of Necessity, a field study that formally identifies conditions within the established boundaries of the area.
2. Develop and adopt a Community Redevelopment Plan. The plan should address the unique needs of the targeted area and include overall goals as well as identify programs and projects
3. Establish a Redevelopment Trust Fund enabling the CRA Board to direct a percentage of property tax revenues to the target areas in order to implement the redevelopment plan.

Once established, the CRA is able to carry out redevelopment and revitalization within designated communities employing the most appropriate use of resources consistent with the public interest. Martin County has seven community redevelopment areas that the CRA oversees: Golden Gate, Hobe Sound, Indiantown, Jensen beach, Old Palm city, Port Salerno and Rio.

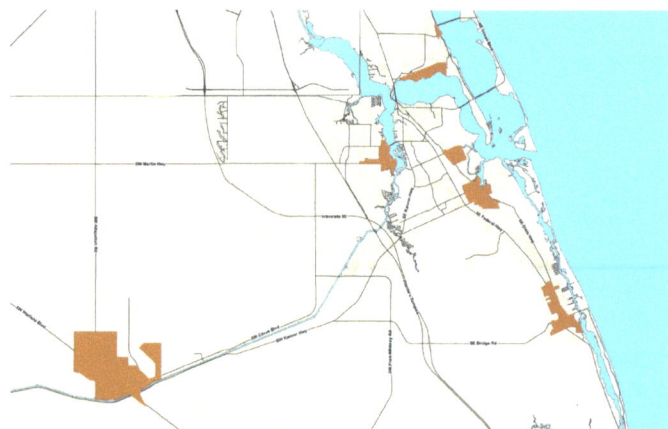

Above: *The overview map highlights the boundaries of the Community Redevelopment Areas in Martin County.*

Above: *Redevelopment Plans attracts private investment.*

Organizational Structure

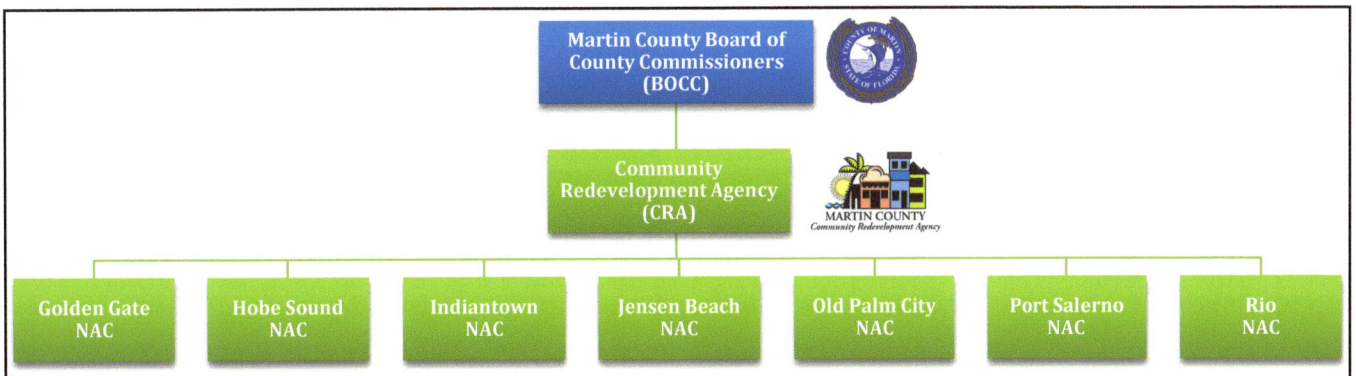

Board of County Commissioners

The Martin County Board of County Commissioners (BOCC) is the Governing body that controls and directs the activities of the Community Redevelopment Agency. The BOCC:

- Sets the amount of TIF received by the CRA (Tax Increment Finance)
- Approves and allocates funds for redevelopment projects.
- Appoints Community Redevelopment Agency members.
- Appoints Neighborhood Advisory Committee members.

Community Redevelopment Agency

The mission of the Martin County Community Redevelopment Agency is "To promote a distinctive community identity and vibrant local economy through inclusive community engagement."
The BOCC has vested limited authority to the Community Redevelopment Agency (CRA) to carry out redevelopment and related activities within the seven designated community redevelopment areas. CRA members oversee that programs and activities are carried out as outlined in the seven Community Redevelopment Plans.

The Martin County Board of County Commissioners, as the governing body, sits as the Community Redevelopment Agency.

Neighborhood Advisory Committee

Each of the Martin County community redevelopment areas has its own Neighborhood Advisory Committee (NAC).

NAC members provide advice and recommendations to the Community Redevelopment Agency regarding the implementation of projects adopted within the Community Redevelopment Plans. This can include the proposal of amendments and modifications to the CRA Plans when needed.

To be appointed as an NAC member, an individual must be either:

1. A resident of the respective community redevelopment area, or
2. A resident of Martin County, who is also a business owner of a business located within the respective Community Redevelopment Area; or
3. A resident of Martin County, who is also a senior manager of a business located within the respective Community Redevelopment Area; or
4. A resident of Martin County, who also owns real property within a half mile of the respective Community Redevelopment Area*.

*No more than two members of any respective Neighborhood Advisory Committee will be appointed from category 4 above.

Neighborhood Advisory Committee Members

In FY14 the Board of County Commissioners appointed the following members of the Neighborhood Advisory Committees to provide advice and recommendations to the Community Redevelopment Agency:

Golden Gate

Jan DalCorso - Joseph Hatton III - Mariann Moore - Althea Redway - Michael Wilchak

Hobe Sound

Nina Gelardi–Angela Hoffman – Gretchen Reich – Luis Reyneri – Charlene Oakowsky
Langdon Parks, Sr. - Michael Banas – Donald Foley

Indiantown

Craig Bauzenberger Sr. - Donna Carman - Catherine Deninger - John (Art) Matson - Bernice Simpson

Jensen Beach

Sharon Adams - Glenda Burgess - Stephen Dutcher - Maria Lindberg - Robert McElroy
Frank Wacha Jr. - Charles Rasmussen - Cynthia Hall

Palm City

Craig Ahal – Joseph Gilio – Jane Landrum – Douglas Legler – Thomas Plymale – Mike Searle
Tracy Seegott - Rex Sentell – Chuck Smith

Port Salerno

Ellan Asselin - Gloria Burns McHardy - Cynthia Oakowsky - Edward Olsen Jr.
Catherine Winters - Karen Worden

Rio

Myra Galoci – Debra Harsh – Sue Kloosterman – Jim Lopilato – Jill Pinkham – Robert Taylor
M. Brent Waddell – David Wishart – Richard Zurich

Community Development Department

The staff of the Community Development Department acts as the liaison between the Board of County Commissioners, Community Redevelopment Agency, the Neighborhood Advisory Committees (NAC) =0and local citizens. In addition, this small team provides administrative, planning, zoning, urban design, and community outreach services to the seven community redevelopment areas.

Kevin Freeman - Director is a professional Town Planner and member of the Royal Town Planning Institute, educated in England he has worked in several communities throughout the United States over the past six years. He brings a specialty interest in sustainability and an approach that seeks to integrate sustainability with community design, transportation impact and local economic development. Prior to this position he was the Development Director at the City of Stuart Fl. and the Assistant Director of Development at Castle Rock CO. He brings significant project management experience to the table from his time as the Acquisition and Planning manager of a private consultancy working with T-Mobile in the UK. Kevin holds a Masters in Urban and Regional Planning from Sheffield Hallam University (England) and a Diploma Town Planning from Sheffield City Polytechnic

Edward Erfurt - Urban Designer is a trained architect and is currently the urban designer for the seven Neighborhood Planning Areas in Martin County, Florida. For the past seven years, he has worked around the country integrating urban design and architecture strategies for redeveloping suburban and urban environments that reflect the need to build walkable communities. Edward has developed Pattern Books and Community Vision Books across the country that promote cities, towns, and neighborhoods, which are beautiful and of lasting value. This body of work builds on the unique character that makes the tapestry of place. He holds a Master of Architectural Design and Urbanism from the University of Notre Dame, and a Bachelor of Architecture from the University of Miami.

Nancy Johnson - Community Development Specialist is a Colombian native with international experience in the collection and analysis of market research and strategic planning. Nancy, in addition to her experience in the USA, has worked in South America, and Europe. This experience specialized in the development of marketing plans to maximize market opportunities and contribute to company promotion and growth. Nancy holds a Masters in Marketing and Market Research with specialty in Marketing Communication from the Universidad de Valencia in Valencia, Spain, and a Bachelor in Business Administration from the Universidad del Norte in Barranquilla, Colombia.

Pinal Gandhi-Savdas - Community Development Specialist is a passionate administrator with over 14 years of professional experience in the management of complex collaborative offices. Pinal is experienced in both public and private sector organizations where she utilized her analytical skills to identify patterns and facilitate problem solving. Pinal holds a Bachelor of Science Degree in Business Administration with a Major in General Business from the University of Central Florida.

Erik Ferguson - Project Engineer is a professional engineer with over 16 years of engineering experience. His work experience ranges from designing major highway and bridge projects for both the New York and North Carolina Department of Transportation, to administration of the Dutchess County Public Works Department in Poughkeepsie, NY. For the past six years Erik has worked as a project engineer with Martin County focusing on traffic signal, traffic calming and intersection improvements. Erik brings an interest in cost effectively creating a sustainable transportation system. Erik holds a Bachelor of Science in Civil Engineering from the University at Buffalo.

Funding Sources

Tax Increment Financing or TIF

The Martin County Community Redevelopment Agency's activities and staff are primarily funded through Tax Increment Financing or TIF.

TIF is a mechanism which captures a percentage of any new tax revenue generated when a vacant or underutilized property is redeveloped. The base year for tax revenue is set as the year in which the community redevelopment area was established. As the majority of redevelopment areas within Martin County were established between 2000 and 2001, the CRA receives a percentage of any tax revenues greater than the amount of revenue captured in those base years.

This percentage can range between 50% and 95%. In fiscal year 2014, the Board of County Commissioners allocated 75% of this increase as TIF funds to be used in the community redevelopment areas.

Generating TIF does not require an additional tax levy or a supplementary assessment on property owners. It is not an additional tax. TIF is one of the tools available to Martin County to leverage funds to promote private sector investment within the primary urban service boundary, and to generate revenues to finance projects.

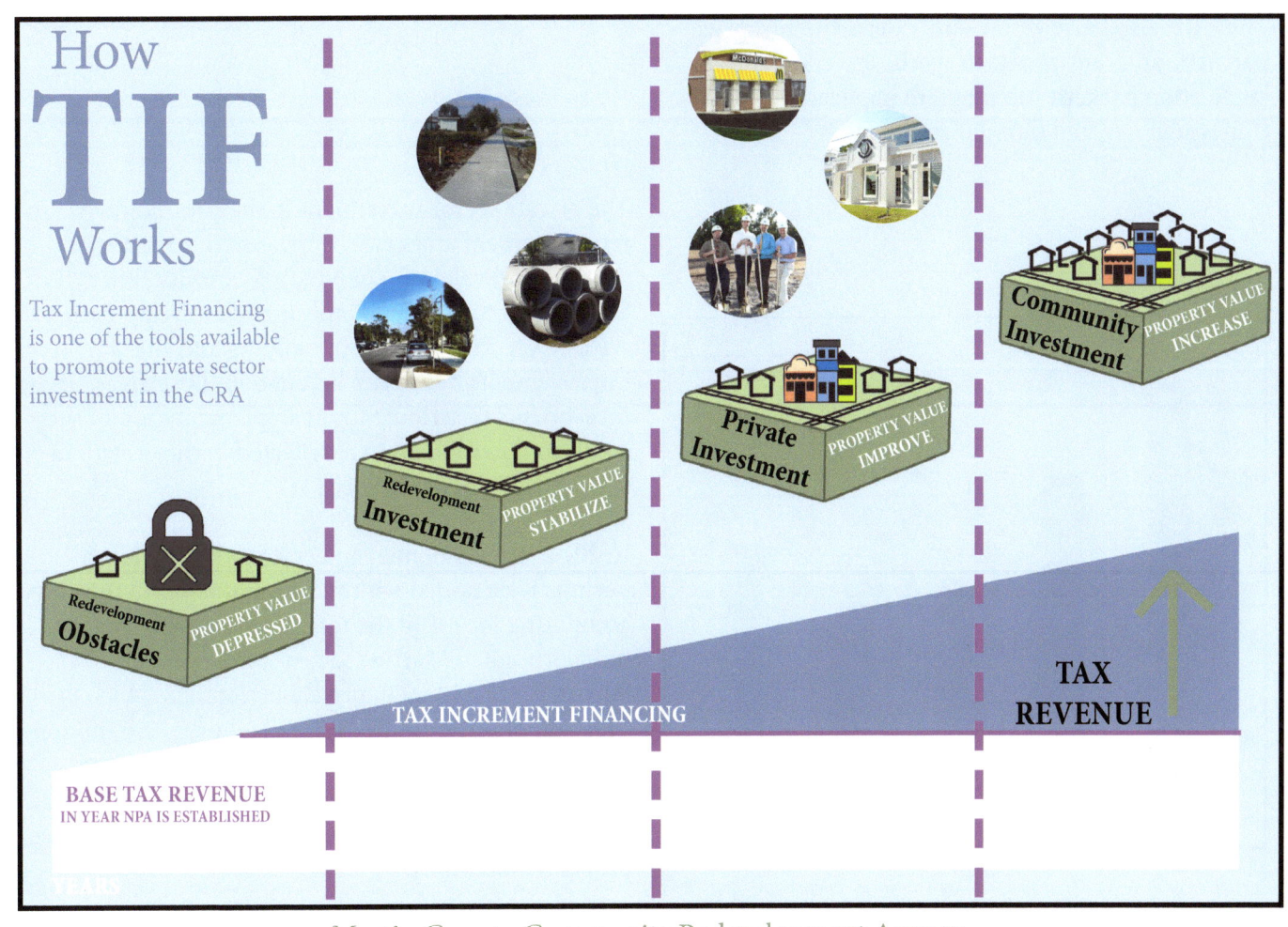

How **TIF** Works

Tax Increment Financing is one of the tools available to promote private sector investment in the CRA

Redevelopment **Obstacles** — PROPERTY VALUE DEPRESSED

Redevelopment **Investment** — PROPERTY VALUE STABILIZE

Private **Investment** — PROPERTY VALUE IMPROVE

Community **Investment** — PROPERTY VALUE INCREASE

TAX INCREMENT FINANCING

TAX REVENUE

BASE TAX REVENUE IN YEAR NPA IS ESTABLISHED

General Funds

The CRA teams with County Departments on many projects throughout the community redevelopment areas. This allows the agency to maximize available Tax Increment Financing (TIF) funds and results in enhanced projects. Contributions by Commissioners utilizing designated district funds also helps in the implementation of projects.

Grants

Community Development Department Staff continuously identifies and pursue appropriate funding opportunities within state, federal, and local agencies to support CRA initiatives. Staff has worked diligently to complete grant applications, gather necessary documents or data, and prepare reports as necessary.

The CRA also liaise with County departments, private partners, and non-profits to synthesize competitive application packets, submit grant applications in a timely manner, and monitor results.

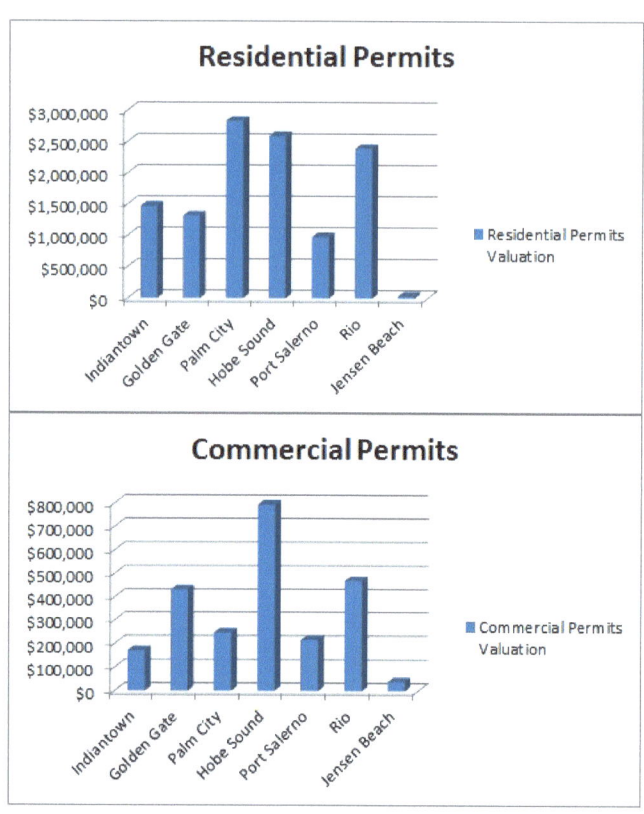

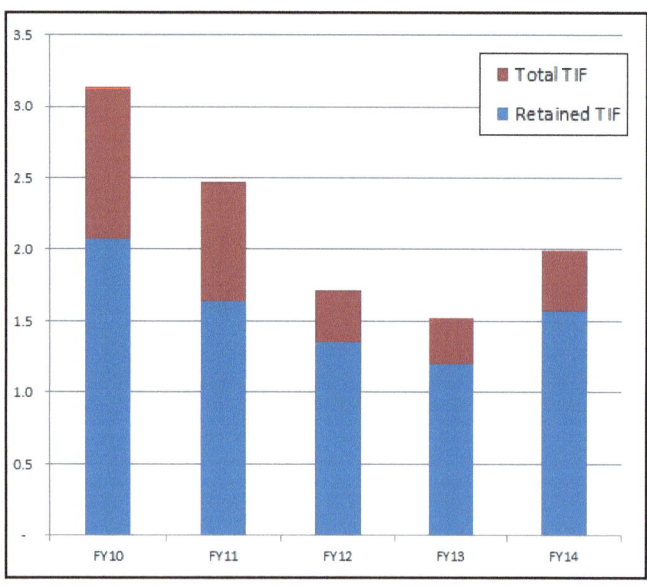

Private Investment

The private sector investment in the community redevelopment areas can be measured through the number and valuation of building permits. Since the adoption of the seven Community Redevelopment Areas, over $340 million in building and site improvements have been invested in those areas. These investments contribute to the implementation of the community vision and are reflected in the growth of the Tax Increment Finance (TIF).

In 2014, 913 residential and commercial building permits were issued within the boundaries of the CRA, accounting for 8% of the total building permits for unincorporated Martin County. These permits totaled $13,977,652.69 in private investment which is a $1.4 million increase from 2013 and over $2.6 million increase from 2012. These permits result in construction, which provides visual evidence of improvement. This private investment will be reflective in next year's property valuations.

CRA Properties

The following are the properties owned by the Martin County CRA at the end of FY14.

Property Address	Redevelopment Area	Acreage
1195 NE Martin Ave	Rio	0.1263
977 NE Dixie Highway	Rio	0.2836
16870 SW Charleston Street	Indiantown	1.0124
1310 NE Dixie Highway	Rio	0.1900
1150 NE Dixie Highway	Rio	0.2583
Unassigned	Port Salerno	0.1520
3254 SE Ellendale St/ 3007 SE Golden Gate Ave.	Golden Gate	0.2020

1150 NE Dixie

16870 SW Charleston

1310 NE Dixie

3007 SE Golden Gate

Unassigned - Port Salerno

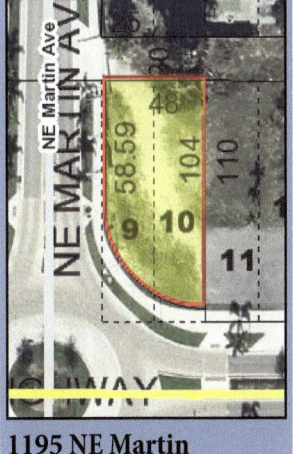

1195 NE Martin

977 NE Dixie

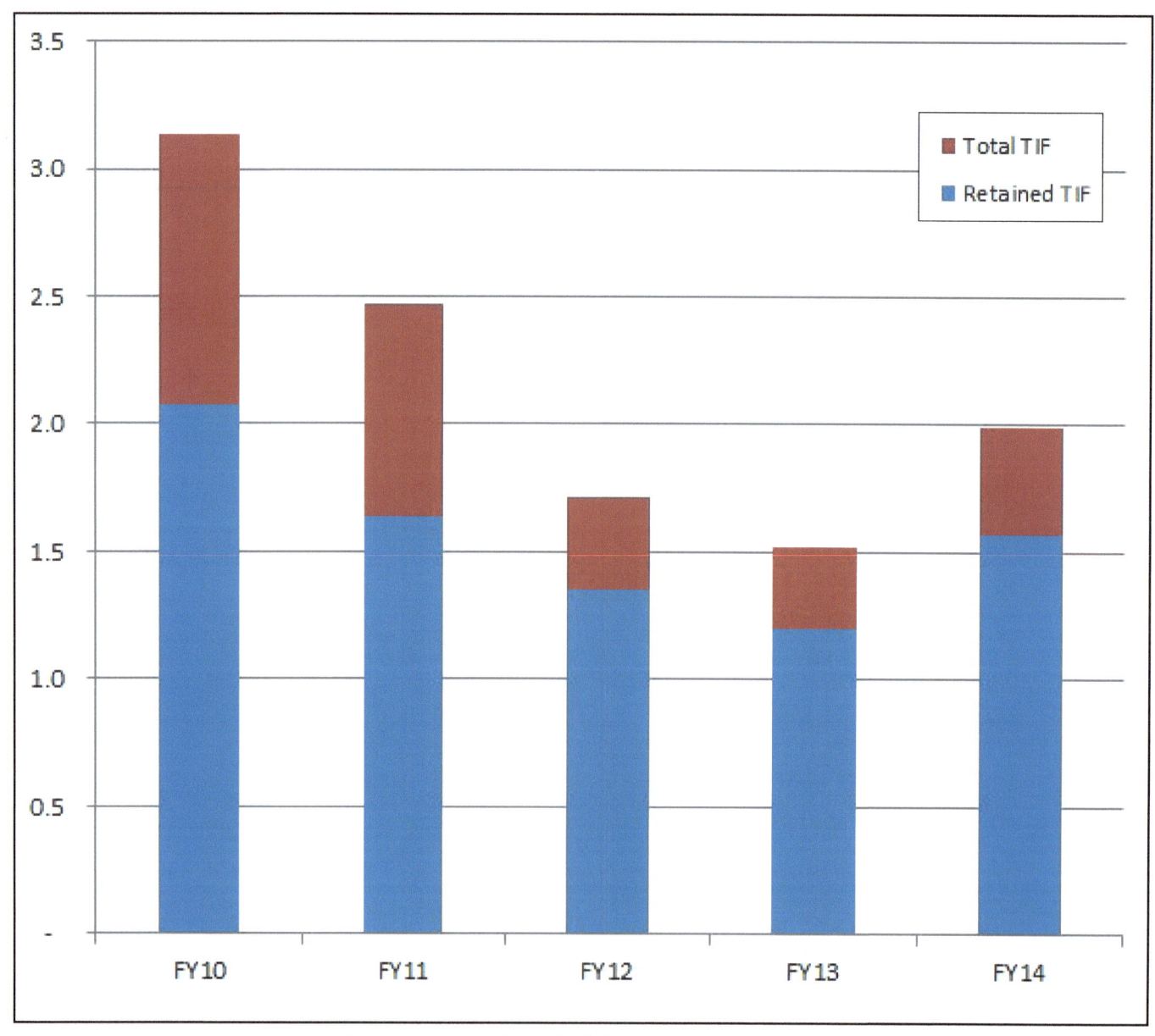

Martin County Board of County Commissioners
Your County, Your Community

Financial Statements

The following are end of year balance sheets for each account held within the Community Redevelopment Trust Fund.

Items of interest:
- Under Liabilities in the Indiantown Trust Fund are funding that was advanced from other Community Redevelopment Area funds and directed towards the Carter Park Affordable Housing/Stormwater Treatment project. These funds are anticipated to be repaid commencing FY16.
- The Community Redevelopment Area Housing Fund is a fund that is dedicated to the implementation of Affordable Housing projects.

CRA Administration

```
                    MARTIN CTY BOARD OF COMMISSIONERS              Page 9
                            BALANCE SHEET                       03/09/2015
                        As of Period 14 Ending                   08:44:30
                        Fiscal Year End 14                       FZGRBALS

                       EXPENDABLE TRUST FUNDS

                       62034 CRA ADMINISTRATION

       Assets
           10103    PCARD CLEARING                            0.00
           10400    EQUITY IN POOLED CASH                10,149.59
           15100    EQUITY IN POOLED INVESTMENTS         76,485.08
           15500    PREPAID ITEMS                             0.00
                                                        _____
                               Total Assets             86,634.67
                                                        ==========

       Liabilities & Equity
         Liabilities
           20103    PCARD CLEARING                            0.00
           20200    ACCOUNTS PAYABLE                        202.04
           21600    ACCRUED WAGES PAYABLE                10,247.79
                                                        _____
                             Total Liabilities          10,449.83

         Equity
           Contributed Capital
           Fund Balance
           24000    Fund Balance/Ret. Earnings Reserved       0.00
           27000    Fund Balance/Ret. Earnings Unreserved 76,184.84
                                                        _____
                 Total Fund Balance/ Retained Earnings  76,184.84
                                                        _____
                 Total Liabilities & Equity                  0.00
                                                        ==========
```

Golden Gate

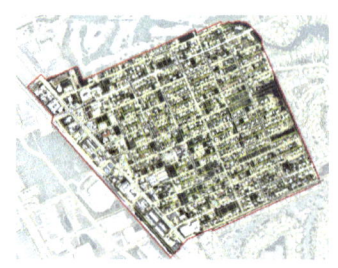

```
                    MARTIN CTY BOARD OF COMMISSIONERS                    Page 5
                              BALANCE SHEET                          03/09/2015
                         As of Period 14 Ending                       08:44:30
                           Fiscal Year End 14                         FZGRBALS

                         EXPENDABLE TRUST FUNDS

                        62024 GOLDEN GATE CRA  FUND
```

Assets

10102	E PAYABLES CLEARING	0.00
10103	PCARD CLEARING	0.00
10400	EQUITY IN POOLED CASH	61.89
13100	DUE FROM OTHER FUNDS	0.00
13290	ADVANCES TO OTHER FUNDS	120,000.00
14200	INVENTORY - FOR RESALE	35,000.00
14210	INVENTORY - FOR RESALE - ENTERPRISE	0.00
15100	EQUITY IN POOLED INVESTMENTS	264,773.82
15500	PREPAID ITEMS	0.00
	Total Assets	**419,835.71**

Liabilities & Equity

Liabilities

20102	E PAYABLES CLEARING	0.00
20103	PCARD CLEARING	0.00
20200	ACCOUNTS PAYABLE	10,075.84
20501	CONTRACTS PAYABLE-RETAINAGE	0.00
21600	ACCRUED WAGES PAYABLE	0.00
	Total Liabilities	**10,075.84**

Equity
Contributed Capital
Fund Balance

24000	Fund Balance/Ret. Earnings Reserved	0.00
27000	Fund Balance/Ret. Earnings Unreserved	409,759.87
	Total Fund Balance/ Retained Earnings	**409,759.87**
	Total Liabilities & Equity	**0.00**

Hobe Sound

```
                     MARTIN CTY BOARD OF COMMISSIONERS              Page 3
                             BALANCE SHEET                        03/09/2015
                          As of Period 14 Ending                   08:44:30
                           Fiscal Year End 14                      FZGRBALS

                          EXPENDABLE TRUST FUNDS

                        62022 HOBE SOUND CRA TRUST FUND
```

Assets

Code	Description	Amount
10102	E PAYABLES CLEARING	0.00
10103	PCARD CLEARING	0.00
10400	EQUITY IN POOLED CASH	16,688.66
13100	DUE FROM OTHER FUNDS	0.00
13290	ADVANCES TO OTHER FUNDS	38,943.00
15100	EQUITY IN POOLED INVESTMENTS	1,121,774.15
15500	PREPAID ITEMS	0.00
	Total Assets	**1,177,405.81**

Liabilities & Equity

Liabilities

Code	Description	Amount
20102	E PAYABLES CLEARING	0.00
20103	PCARD CLEARING	0.00
20200	ACCOUNTS PAYABLE	26,645.75
20501	CONTRACTS PAYABLE-RETAINAGE	0.00
20700	DUE TO OTHER FUNDS	0.00
21600	ACCRUED WAGES PAYABLE	0.00
23690	ADVANCES FROM OTHER FUNDS	0.00
	Total Liabilities	**26,645.75**

Equity

Contributed Capital

Fund Balance

Code	Description	Amount
24000	Fund Balance/Ret. Earnings Reserved	0.00
27000	Fund Balance/Ret. Earnings Unreserved	1,150,760.06
	Total Fund Balance/ Retained Earnings	**1,150,760.06**
	Total Liabilities & Equity	**0.00**

Indiantown

```
                    MARTIN CTY BOARD OF COMMISSIONERS              Page 6
                              BALANCE SHEET                     03/09/2015
                          As of Period 14 Ending                 08:44:30
                           Fiscal Year End 14                    FZGRBALS

                          EXPENDABLE TRUST FUNDS

                        62025 INDIANTOWN CRA  FUND

    Assets
        10102   E PAYABLES CLEARING                          0.00
        10103   PCARD CLEARING                               0.00
        10400   EQUITY IN POOLED CASH                   29,718.22
        10425   POOLED CASH/CARTER PARK PROJECT              0.00
        14200   INVENTORY - FOR RESALE                  38,063.94
        14210   INVENTORY - FOR RESALE - ENTERPRISE          0.00
        15100   EQUITY IN POOLED INVESTMENTS                 0.00
        15500   PREPAID ITEMS                                0.00
                                                       _____
                                Total Assets             67,782.16
                                                       ============

    Liabilities & Equity
      Liabilities
        20102   E PAYABLES CLEARING                          0.00
        20103   PCARD CLEARING                               0.00
        20200   ACCOUNTS PAYABLE                         8,702.00
        21600   ACCRUED WAGES PAYABLE                        0.00
        23690   ADVANCES FROM OTHER FUNDS              674,296.00
                                                       _____
                            Total Liabilities          682,998.00

      Equity
        Contributed Capital
        Fund Balance
        24000   Fund Balance/Ret. Earnings Reserved         0.00
        27000   Fund Balance/Ret. Earnings Unreserved  <  615,215.84>
                                                       _____
                Total Fund Balance/ Retained Earnings  <  615,215.84>

                      Total Liabilities & Equity               0.00
                                                       ============
```

Under Liabilities in the Indiantown Trust Fund are funding that was advanced from other Community Redevelopment Area funds and directed towards the Carter Park Affordable Housing/Stormwater Treatment project. These funds are anticipated to be repaid commencing FY16.

Jensen Beach

```
                MARTIN CTY BOARD OF COMMISSIONERS              Page 1
                           BALANCE SHEET                     03/09/2015
                      As of Period 14 Ending                  08:44:30
                       Fiscal Year End 14                     FZGRBALS

                      EXPENDABLE TRUST FUNDS

                 6202 JENSEN BEACH CRA TRUST FUND

  Assets
     10103   PCARD CLEARING                                       0.00
     10400   EQUITY IN POOLED CASH                            21,485.39
     15100   EQUITY IN POOLED INVESTMENTS                    136,067.18
     15500   PREPAID ITEMS                                        0.00
                                                         _____
                                    Total Assets            157,552.57
                                                         ══════════════

  Liabilities & Equity
    Liabilities
     20103   PCARD CLEARING                                       0.00
     20200   ACCOUNTS PAYABLE                                     0.00
     21600   ACCRUED WAGES PAYABLE                                0.00
                                                         _____
                                 Total Liabilities                0.00
    Equity
      Contributed Capital
      Fund Balance
     24000   Fund Balance/Ret. Earnings Reserved                 0.00
     27000   Fund Balance/Ret. Earnings Unreserved        157,552.57
                                                         _____
              Total Fund Balance/ Retained Earnings        157,552.57
                                                         _____
                       Total Liabilities & Equity                0.00
                                                         ══════════════
```

Old Palm City

```
            MARTIN CTY BOARD OF COMMISSIONERS                    Page  7
                     BALANCE SHEET                            03/09/2015
                  As of Period 14 Ending                        08:44:30
                    Fiscal Year End 14                          FZGRBALS

                  EXPENDABLE TRUST FUNDS

                62026 PALM CITY CRA   FUND
```

Assets

10102	E PAYABLES CLEARING	0.00
10103	PCARD CLEARING	0.00
10400	EQUITY IN POOLED CASH	51,343.08
15100	EQUITY IN POOLED INVESTMENTS	1,407,172.42
15500	PREPAID ITEMS	0.00
	Total Assets	**1,458,515.50**

Liabilities & Equity

Liabilities

20102	E PAYABLES CLEARING	149.77
20103	PCARD CLEARING	0.00
20200	ACCOUNTS PAYABLE	50,211.22
21600	ACCRUED WAGES PAYABLE	0.00
	Total Liabilities	**50,360.99**

Equity

Contributed Capital

Fund Balance

24000	Fund Balance/Ret. Earnings Reserved	0.00
27000	Fund Balance/Ret. Earnings Unreserved	1,408,154.51
	Total Fund Balance/ Retained Earnings	**1,408,154.51**
	Total Liabilities & Equity	**0.00**

Port Salerno

MARTIN CTY BOARD OF COMMISSIONERS
BALANCE SHEET
As of Period 14 Ending
Fiscal Year End 14

EXPENDABLE TRUST FUNDS

62023 PORT SALERNO CRA TRUST FUND

Assets

10102	E PAYABLES CLEARING	0.00
10103	PCARD CLEARING	0.00
10400	EQUITY IN POOLED CASH	20,896.56
13290	ADVANCES TO OTHER FUNDS	124,568.00
14200	INVENTORY - FOR RESALE	1,330.00
15100	EQUITY IN POOLED INVESTMENTS	1,375,432.93
15500	PREPAID ITEMS	0.00
	Total Assets	**1,522,227.49**

Liabilities & Equity

Liabilities

20102	E PAYABLES CLEARING	0.00
20103	PCARD CLEARING	0.00
20200	ACCOUNTS PAYABLE	25,578.84
20501	CONTRACTS PAYABLE-RETAINAGE	0.00
21600	ACCRUED WAGES PAYABLE	0.00
	Total Liabilities	**25,578.84**

Equity

Contributed Capital

Fund Balance

24000	Fund Balance/Ret. Earnings Reserved	0.00
27000	Fund Balance/Ret. Earnings Unreserved	1,496,648.65
	Total Fund Balance/ Retained Earnings	**1,496,648.65**
	Total Liabilities & Equity	**0.00**

Rio

```
                    MARTIN CTY BOARD OF COMMISSIONERS                    Page 2
                            BALANCE SHEET                              03/09/2015
                        As of Period 14 Ending                         08:44:30
                          Fiscal Year End 14                           FZGRBALS

                        EXPENDABLE TRUST FUNDS

                        62021 RIO CRA TRUST FUND
```

Assets

10102	E PAYABLES CLEARING	0.00
10103	PCARD CLEARING	0.00
10400	EQUITY IN POOLED CASH	82.91
13290	ADVANCES TO OTHER FUNDS	390,785.00
15100	EQUITY IN POOLED INVESTMENTS	514,737.37
15500	PREPAID ITEMS	0.00
	Total Assets	**905,605.28**

Liabilities & Equity

Liabilities

20102	E PAYABLES CLEARING	295.94
20103	PCARD CLEARING	0.00
20200	ACCOUNTS PAYABLE	115,099.13
20501	CONTRACTS PAYABLE-RETAINAGE	0.00
20700	DUE TO OTHER FUNDS	0.00
21600	ACCRUED WAGES PAYABLE	0.00
	Total Liabilities	**115,395.07**

Equity

Contributed Capital

Fund Balance

24000	Fund Balance/Ret. Earnings Reserved	0.00
27000	Fund Balance/Ret. Earnings Unreserved	790,210.21
	Total Fund Balance/ Retained Earnings	**790,210.21**
	Total Liabilities & Equity	**0.00**

CRA Housing

```
                    MARTIN CTY BOARD OF COMMISSIONERS            Page 10
                              BALANCE SHEET                    03/09/2015
                        As of Period 14 Ending                  08:44:30
                          Fiscal Year End 14                    FZGRBALS

                        EXPENDABLE TRUST FUNDS

                          62035 CRA HOUSING

   Assets
        10400    EQUITY IN POOLED CASH                   584.56
        15100    EQUITY IN POOLED INVESTMENTS         33,950.63
                                                       _____
                               Total Assets           34,535.19
                                                       =========

   Liabilities & Equity
      Liabilities
        20200    ACCOUNTS PAYABLE                          0.00
        20501    CONTRACTS PAYABLE-RETAINAGE               0.00
                                                       _____
                            Total Liabilities             0.00

      Equity
        Contributed Capital
        Fund Balance
        24000    Fund Balance/Ret. Earnings Reserved       0.00
        27000    Fund Balance/Ret. Earnings Unreserved 34,535.19
                                                       _____
               Total Fund Balance/ Retained Earnings  34,535.19

                       Total Liabilities & Equity          0.00
                                                       =========
```

The Community Redevelopment Area Housing Fund is a fund that is dedicated to the implementation of Affordable Housing projects.

Martin County Board of County Commissioners
Your County, Your Community

FY14 CRA Projects

Area Summary

CRA Areas:
- Golden Gate
- Hobe Sound
- Indiantown
- Jensen Beach
- Old Palm City
- Port Salerno
- Rio

Plan Adoptions: 2001-2002

Total Area:
- 8,565.5 Total Acres
- 2.4% of Martin County

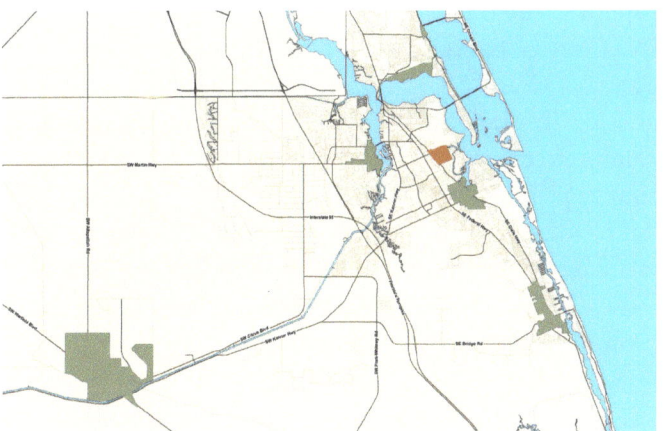

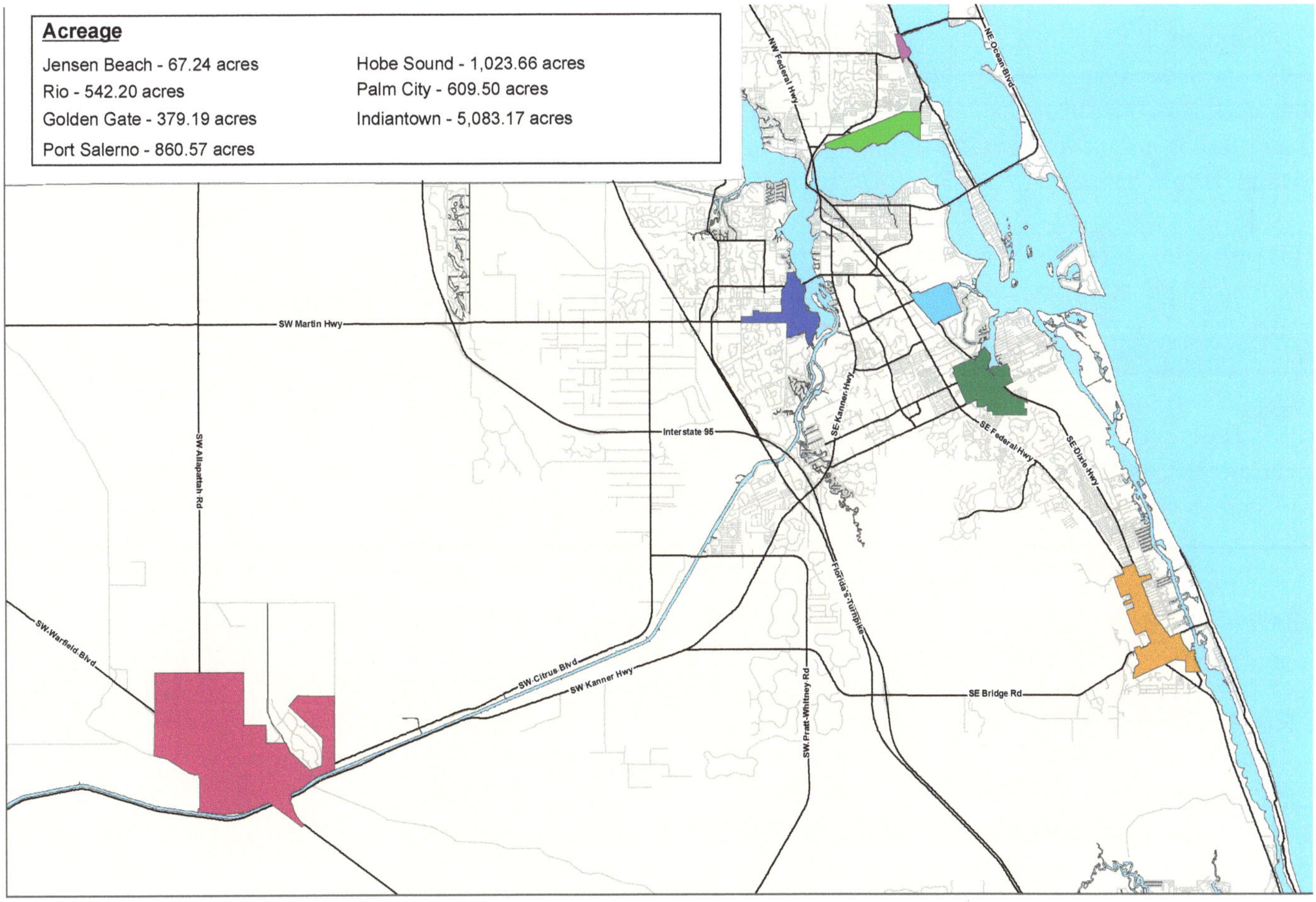

Acreage

Jensen Beach - 67.24 acres	Hobe Sound - 1,023.66 acres
Rio - 542.20 acres	Palm City - 609.50 acres
Golden Gate - 379.19 acres	Indiantown - 5,083.17 acres
Port Salerno - 860.57 acres	

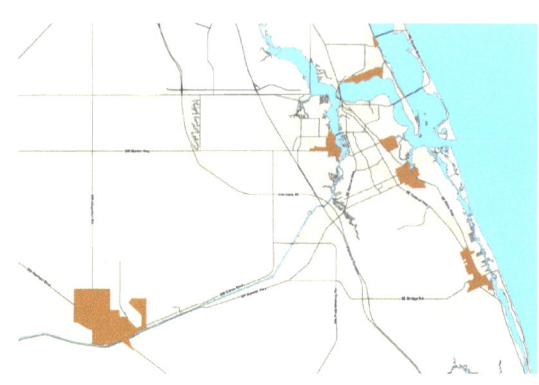

Redevelopment Technical Assistance

The mission of the Community Redevelopment Agency is to promote a distinctive community identity and vibrant local economy which is supported by the Community Redevelopment Plans and Overlay Land Development Regulations. The Board of County Commissioners supports this mission through Policy 4.2B.3 of the Martin County Comprehensive Growth Management Plan which the county provides technical, planning resources to aid the residents and landowners with redevelopment and in-fill development. The CRA planning staff actively engages property owners and development teams throughout the development process.

The Community Development Department Staff is composed of professionals with the education and experience in the fields of planning, architecture, and engineering, and a working institutional knowledge of Martin County's Comprehensive Plan, Land Development Regulations, and Permitting Processes. This experience provides a competitive advantage that attracts private investment in the CRA, while championing and promoting the community vision with each new development.

This process has resulted in numerous successful Site Plan Applications reviewed and approved under expedited processing through the County's Development Review Process. This has also led to a concentrated number of building permits within the CRA. These results are attracting new investment, creating jobs, and adding taxable value to the community redevelopment areas.

Project Type:
- Redevelopment
- Economic Development

Funding Source:
- Staff Allocation

Status: On-going

Project Manager: Edward W. Erfurt

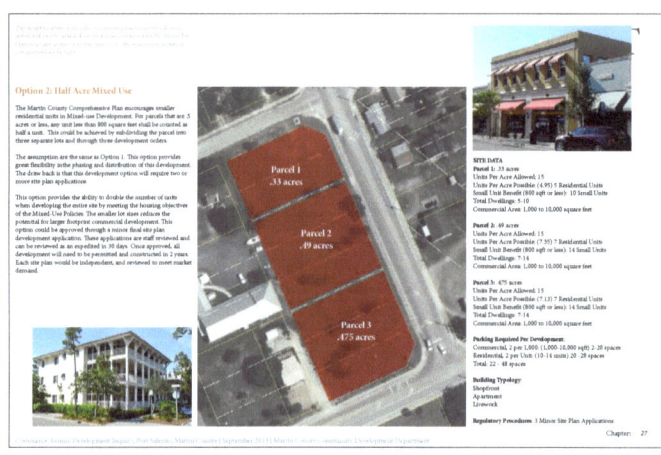

Design Review & Permitting

The Community Redevelopment Agency provides professional technical services to the public, the Martin County Growth Management Department, and the Martin County Building Department, to promote a distinctive community identity throughout the seven community redevelopment areas while supporting a vibrant local economy.

Staff provides technical support to property owners within the CRA boundaries by familiarizing owners with development requirements and illustrating how regulations may be applied to their specific site. This hands-on approach involves pro-actively meeting with the developer of a site to understand their desires and connect them to the community's vision. Once an applicant begins the formal development process, staff serves as an advocate for the project and assists in moving the application through required review in an expeditious manner.

Staff also meets with professionals in the field of architecture, construction, and real estate to educate and promote redevelopment and investment within the redevelopment areas.

As a member of the Martin County's Development Review Team, staff participates in the permit review of development and building applications within the CRA. Staff is able to act as voice for residents through these permits. In addition, the Urban Designer reviews all commercial development applications County-wide.

In FY2014 there were a total of 913 building permits issued in the CRA. This accounts for 8% of the total building permits in Martin County with a valuation of $13.9 million dollars. This is a 11% increase in the valuation invested through building permits by the private sector in the Community Redevelopment Areas from the previous year.

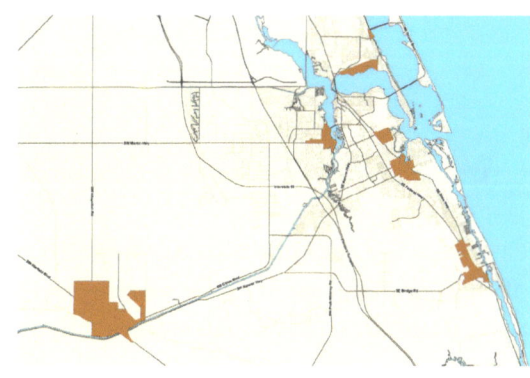

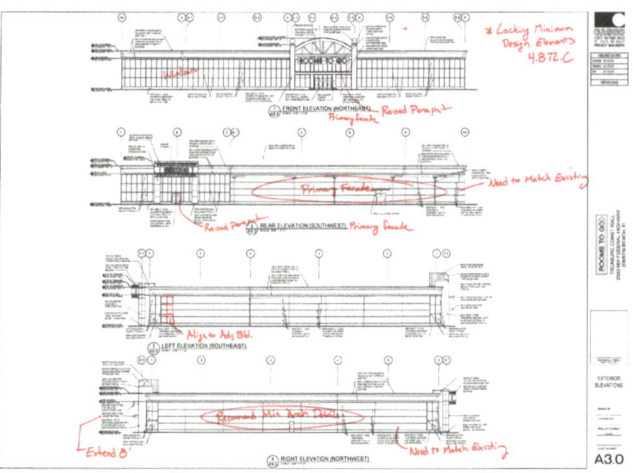

Project Type:
- Redevelopment
- Urban Design Review
- Permitting

Funding Source:
- Staff Allocation

Status: On-going

Project Manager: Edward W. Erfurt

Community Oriented Code

Currently the community redevelopment areas consist of eight (8) different Land Development Regulations, five (5) different Architectural Design Requirements, and two (2) separate parking studies. In addition to these regulations, new code provisions have been added to the Martin County Land Development Regulations.

These governing regulations were developed independently over several years by various consultant teams. As a result, there is often inconsistency in the language and content of these regulations, resulting in frustration, confusion, and a complicated development review and permitting process.

In an effort to streamline the development process the CRA is currently working with a qualified consultant to establish a unifying visually based code for all seven community redevelopment areas.

In collaboration with the community and the Growth Management Department, staff has outlined all of the performance standards currently regulated in all of the existing codes, and identified where duplication can be eliminated. Staff is working with Growth Management, Engineering, and the Legal Department, to integrate Parking, Roadway, Landscaping, and Signage requirements in the code.

Staff began the preparations to present the proposed changes to the redevelopment areas and neighborhood advisory committees. These proposed revisions will be the focus of numerous public workshops and presented to the Board of County Commissions in 2014 for adoption.

Project Type:
- Zoning and Community

Planning Funding Source:
- Tax Increment Finance $198,000

Status: In progress

Project Manager: Edward W. Erfurt

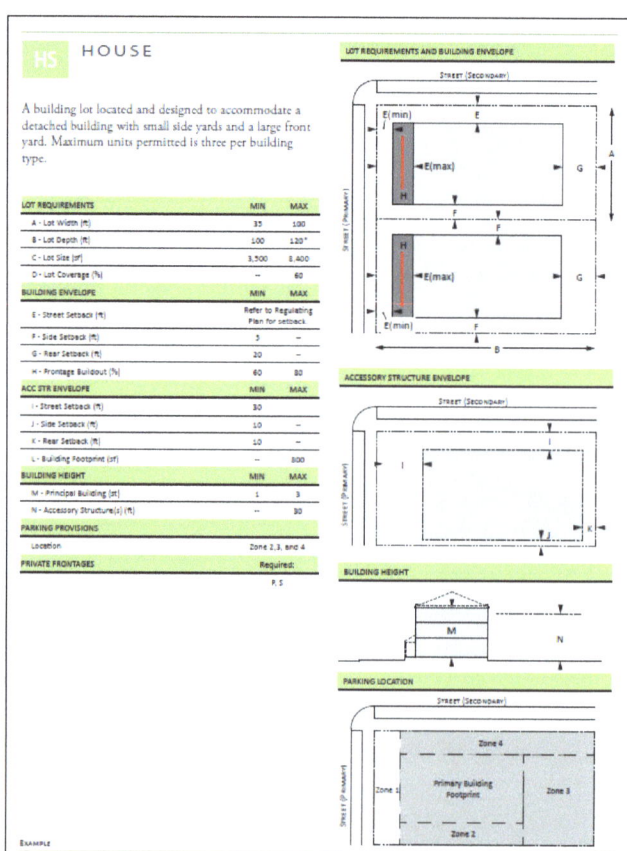

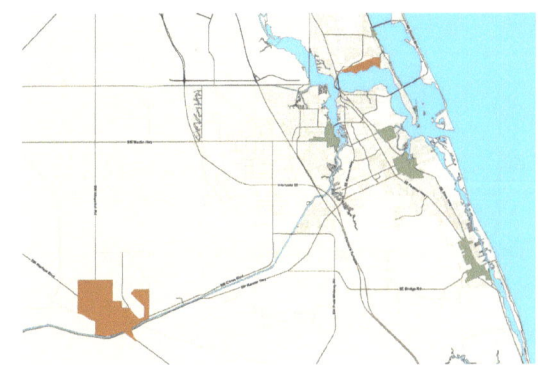

CRA Property Acquisition

As contemplated in both, Florida Statutes and Community Redevelopment Plan, the Community Redevelopment Agency may acquire property within a slum or blighted area by purchase, lease, option, gift, grant, bequest, devise, or other voluntary method of acquisition to meet the goals and objectives of the Community Redevelopment Plan.

In FY14 the Community Redevelopment Agency coordinated with the Building's Department Code Enforcement Division and Engineering's Department Property Management Division, the acquisition of properties subject to multiple code enforcement fines and as part of roadway improvement projects.

The following are the properties owned by the Martin County CRA at the end of FY14.

Property Address	Redevelopment Area	Acreage
1195 NE Martin Ave	Rio	0.1263
977 NE Dixie Highway	Rio	0.2836
16870 SW Charleston Street	Indiantown	1.0124
1310 NE Dixie Highway	Rio	0.1900
1150 NE Dixie Highway	Rio	0.2583
Unassigned	Port Salerno	0.1520
3254 SE Ellendale St/ 3007 SE Golden Gate Ave.	Golden Gate	0.2020

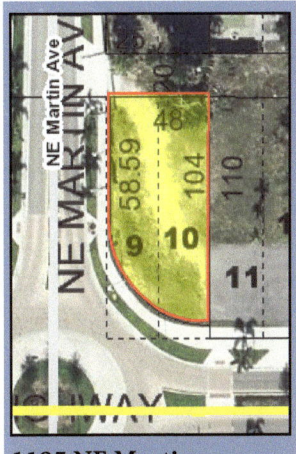

1195 NE Martin

977 NE Dixie

16870 SW Charleston

1150 NE Dixie

Unassigned - Port Salerno

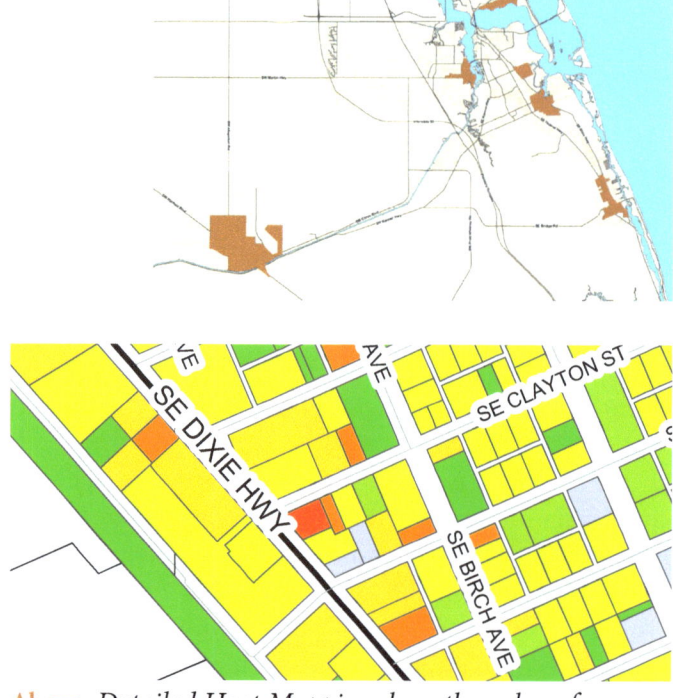

Property Appraisal Evaluation

The Community Redevelopment Agency annually maps the appraised and taxable property values as assigned by the Martin County Property Appraiser in each of the redevelopment areas. These maps illustrate the wealth and productivity found in the community redevelopment areas. Staff is also able to evaluate the property tax implications of different development types and the return on investment for capital projects.

According to the Property Appraiser, the seven Martin County Community Redevelopment Areas have a combined appraised value of $1.1 billion, of which $736 million is taxable. The CRA encompasses 8,500 acres of land mass or about 3% of the County. The value of taxable of the land within the CRA is some of the most productive land representing over 5% of the total taxable value for Martin County.

Above: Detailed Heat Mapping show the value of traditional development patterns and the return on investment from both the public and private sector.

These evaluations illustrate the total property value per acre per parcel throughout each redevelopment area. Over several years of this mapping, staff is able to reflect and compare the growth in these land values which provides real data for future investment and growth in the redevelopment areas.

Project Type:
- Analysis
- Forecasting

Funding Source:
- Staff Allocation

Status: On-going

Project Manager: Edward W. Erfurt

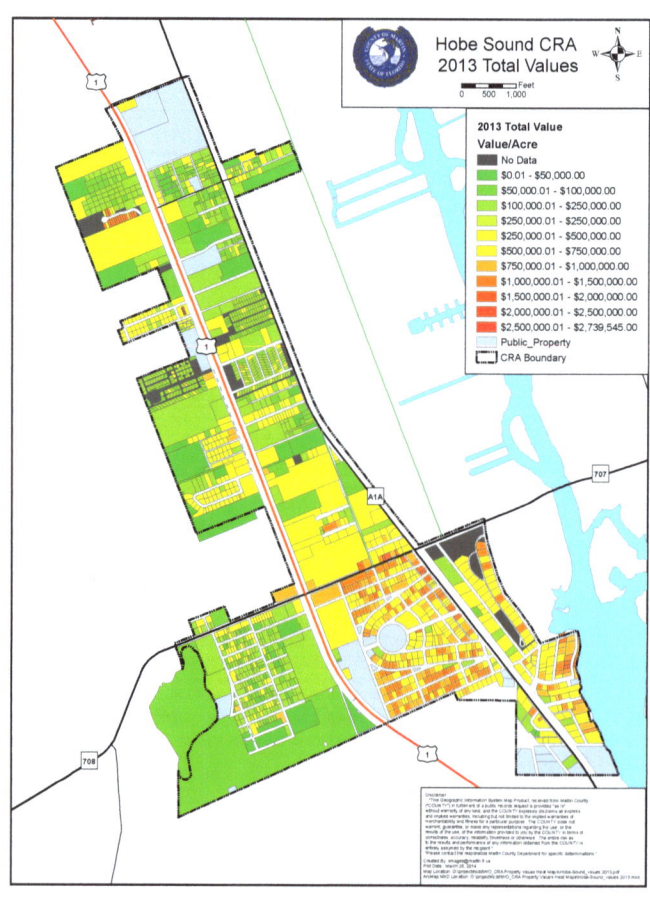

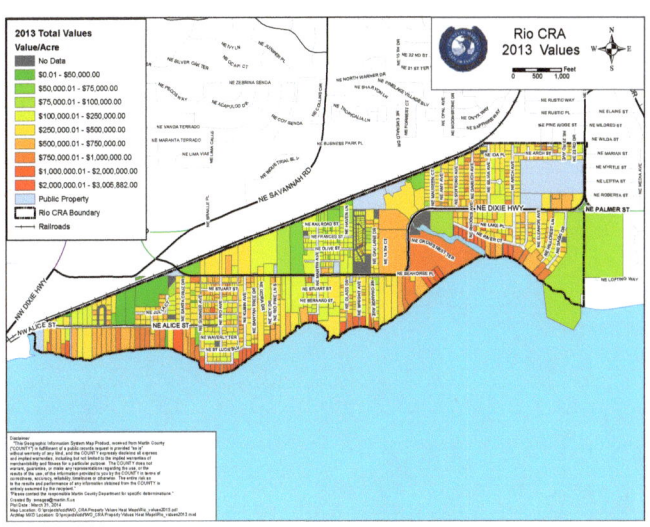

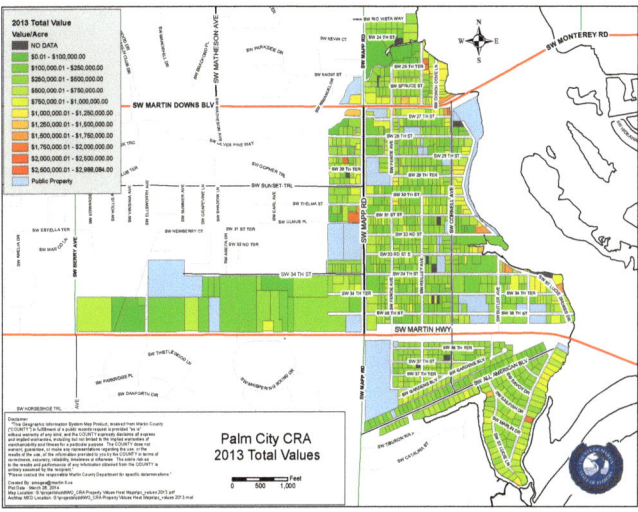

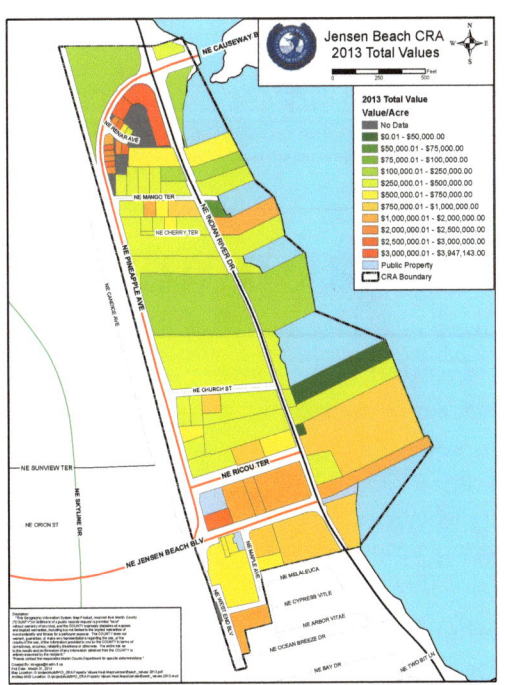

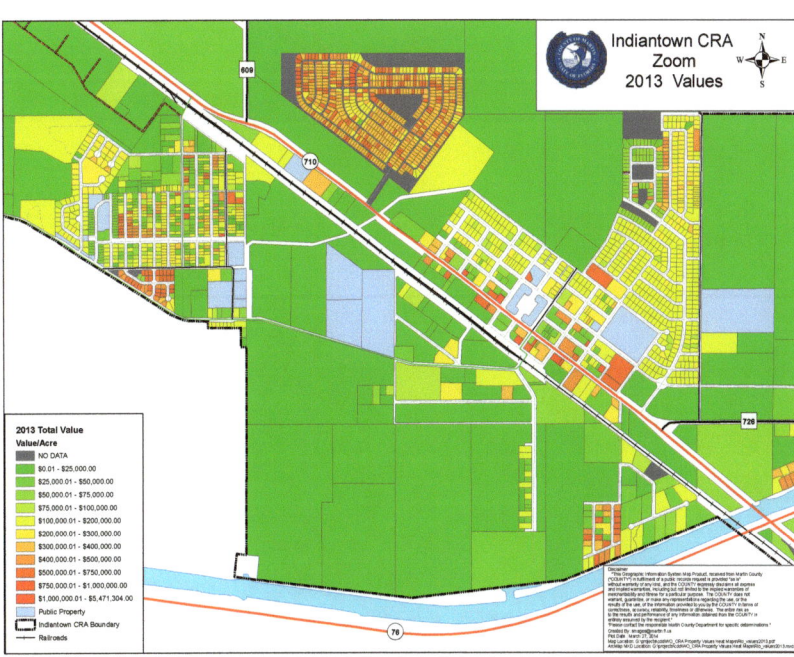

Area Summary

CRA Area: Golden Gate

Plan Adoption: September 2002

Total Area: 379 Acres

Area Highlights:

- Proximity to Witham Field Airport
- Access to FEC Rail

Special Designations:

- Neighborhood Stabilization Program (NSP) Target Area

Golden Gate

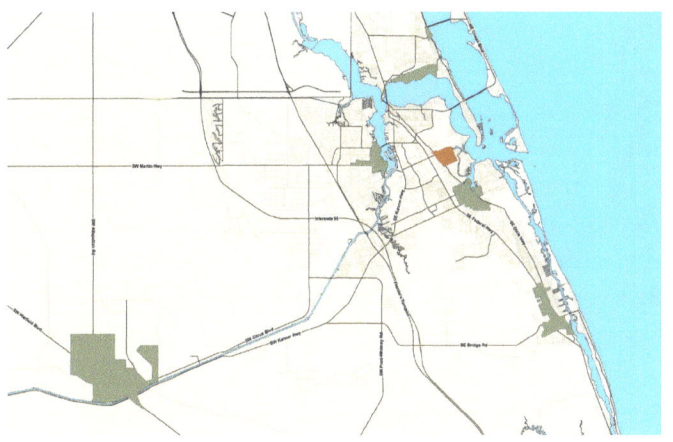

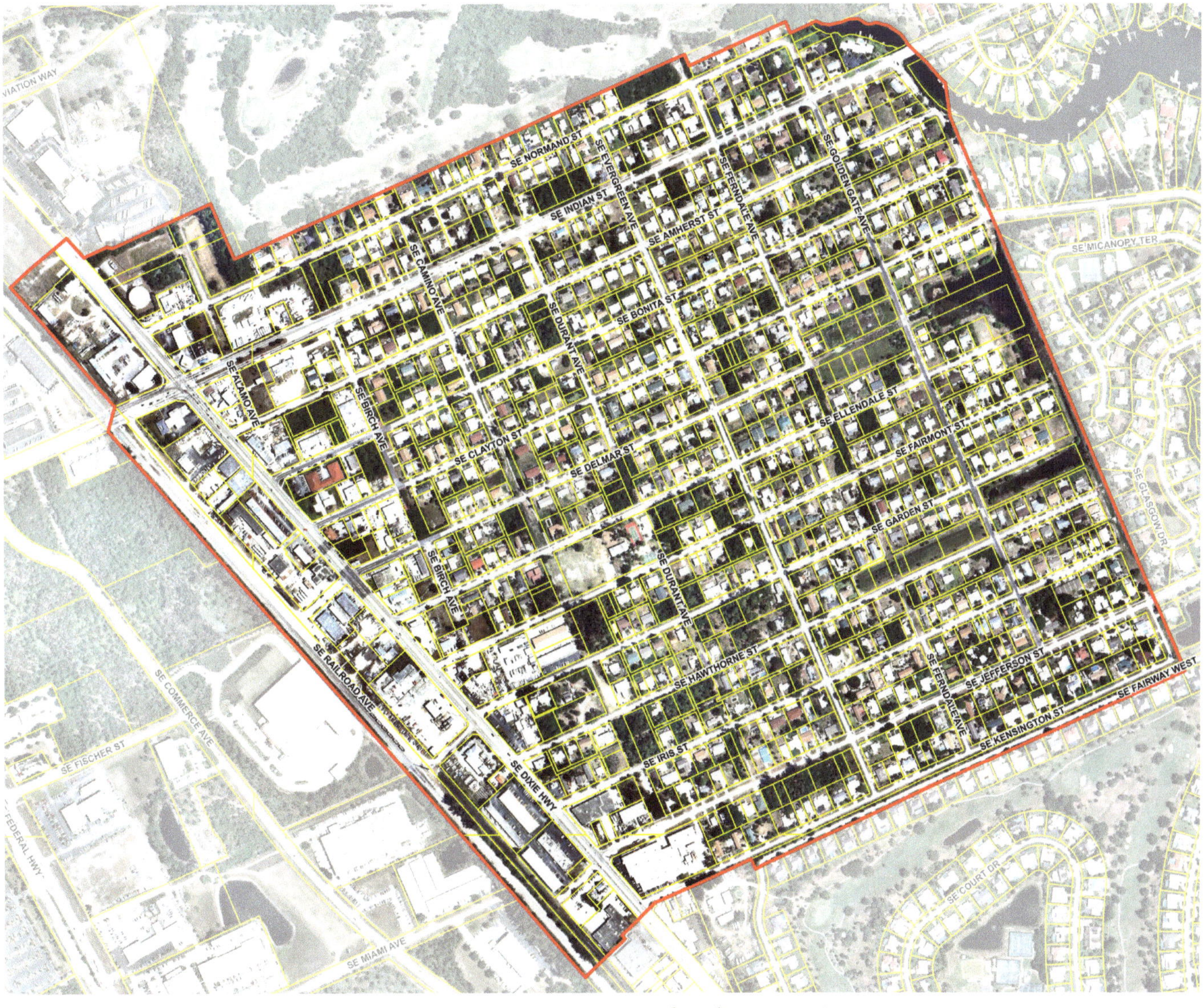

SE NORMAND ST
SE INDIAN ST
SE EVERGREEN AVE
SE AMHERST ST
SE FERNDALE AVE
SE GOLDEN GATE AVE
SE MICANOPY TER
SE CAMINO AVE
SE BONITA ST
SE DURANT AVE
SE ALAMO AVE
SE BIRCH AVE
SE ELLENDALE ST
SE FAIRMONT ST
SE CLAYTON ST
SE DELMAR ST
SE GLASGOW DR
SE GARDEN ST
SE HAWTHORNE ST
SE JEFFERSON ST
SE FAIRWAY WEST
SE RAILROAD AVE
SE COMMERCE AVE
SE KENSINGTON ST
SE IRIS ST
SE DIXIE HWY
SE FISCHER ST
FEDERAL HWY
SE COURT DR
SE MIAMI AVE

Golden Gate Neighborhood Stormwater Retrofit Study

The Golden Gate Neighborhood Stormwater Retrofit Study uses two properties of the neighborhood to make an assessment of the current conditions and identify the potential benefits of using different alternatives to enhance stormwater retention/detention within private properties in the Community Redevelopment Areas.

A stormwater Best Management Practice (BMP) is a method or combination of methods found to be the most effective and feasible means of reducing the amount of pollution generated by developments. There are several different options available for providing additional treatment and storage of stormwater runoff.

The stormwater retrofit study, analyzed several options and determined the most effective and efficient means to address stormwater quality and alleviate minor flooding concerns. The results of the analysis can be replicated on impervious sites that predate the current water quality standards. The study also revealed the presence of a hardpan layer of soil, approximately 12" beneath the bottom of the retention areas that should be removed to allow proper percolation of stormwater into the underlying soils.

The implementation of such alternatives throughout the neighborhood could assist the County in meeting its obligations for water quality improvement mandated Total Maximum Daily Load (TMDL) in the St. Lucie Basin Management Action Plan (BMAP).

Project Type: Innovative Stormwater Management
Funding Source:
- Tax Increment Finance (TIF) $6,000

Status:
- Completed

Project Manager: Erik Ferguson, PE

Property Acquisition & Redevelopment

As contemplated in both, Florida Statutes and Community Redevelopment Plan, the Community Redevelopment Agency may acquire property within a slum or blighted area by purchase, lease, option, gift, grant, bequest, devise, or other voluntary method of acquisition to meet the goals and objectives of the Community Redevelopment Plan.

In FY14 the Community Redevelopment Agency coordinated with the Building's Department Code Enforcement Division and Engineering's Department Property Management Division, the acquisition of a property located within the CRA boundaries in the Golden Gate Neighborhood to assist in the revitalization of the surrounding neighborhood.

In January 2014, the CRA acquired the duplex located at 3007 SE Golden Gate Avenue, and 3254 SE Ellendale Street. The property was subject of ongoing code enforcement action that dates back to 2009 and suffered from fire damage, vandalism, and general neglect.

The CRA is vested by the State of Florida pursuant to its powers under Florida Statutes, Chapter 163, Part III, the Community Redevelopment Act of 1969 as amended, with the authority to request proposals for the redevelopment of any area within its district in order to effectuate redevelopment pursuant to the goals and objectives of the CRA Redevelopment Plan.

Community Development Department staff prepared a Request for Proposals (RFP) for the sale of the property to a qualified proposer that will redevelop the site to further the revitalization of the area and to fulfill the neighborhood's goals for the area as expressed in the Golden Gate Community Redevelopment Plan. Sale of the property is expected to be completed in FY15.

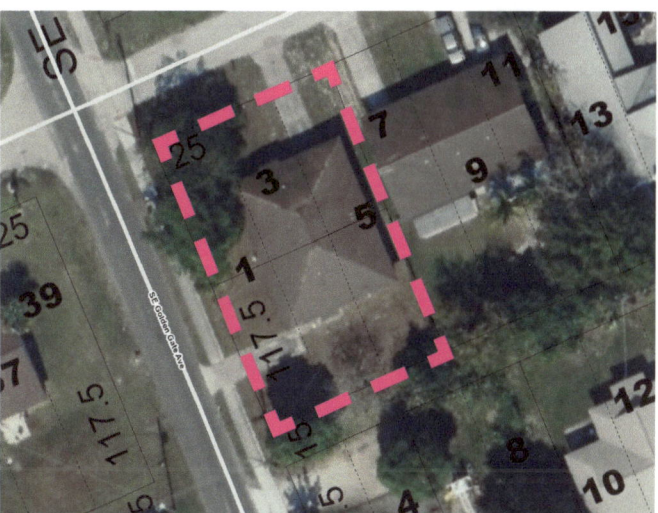

Project Type:
• Property Acquisition and Redevelopment
Proposed Funding Source:
• Tax Increment Financing (TIF)
Status:
• Acquisition process completed
• Request for Proposals advertisement underway
Project Manager: Nancy Johnson

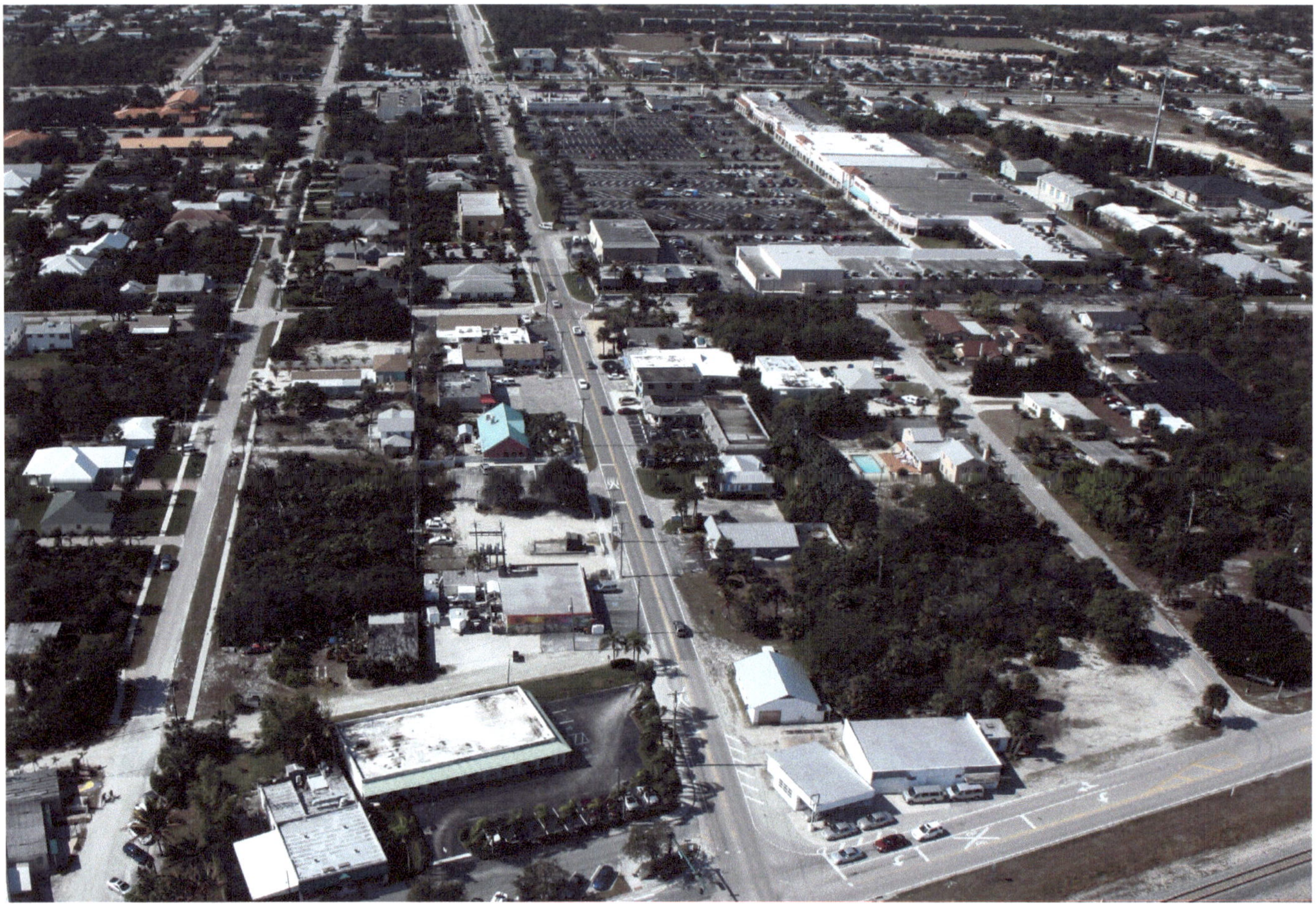

Area Summary

CRA Area: Hobe Sound

Plan Adoption: December 2000

Total Area: 1,024 Acres

Area Highlights:
- Southern Gateway into Martin County from Jupiter Island and Palm Beach
- Access to FEC Rail

Special Designations:
- Mixed-Use Overlay

Hobe Sound

Bridge Road Main Street

Plans to enhance Bridge Road between US-1 and Dixie Highway officially began in 2000 with the establishment of the Hobe Sound Redevelopment Plan. Precursor goals for the corridor were identified as early as 1994. Bridge Road was highlighted as the #1 focus area in the 2010 NOW Visioning community report. The vision for Bridge Road is that of a sustainable neighborhood "Main Street" setting that will support a vibrant downtown for all. Objectives of the Bridge Road project include increasing the amount of on-street parking, improving vehicular and pedestrian safety, undergrounding overhead utilities, improving drainage, reducing speeds, and promoting walkability through sidewalk additions and landscape enhancements.

Staff has worked closely with the Hobe Sound Neighborhood Advisory Committee (NAC) and the community on the corridor design since early 2011. Staff has also engaged with businesses owners and property owners along Bridge Road by hosting open houses and scheduling one-on-one meetings. Participation by the NAC, residents, business owners and property owners ensures the design will meet the individual needs of each business along the corridor and align with the vision as outlined in the Hobe Sound Redevelopment Plan.

Engineering drawings are currently being drafted, accounting for the needs of the property owners and businesses along Bridge Road.

The Martin County Board of County Commissioners have approved the acceptance of any right of way needed to complete the project. Staff is coordinating with property owners and Martin County's Property Management department to accept additional right of way needed to make the project a reality.

The CRA received 90% design plans in July 2014. With $1.1 million available in TIF for construction, the CRA will phase the project that aligns with the available TIF dollars.

Project Type:
- Complete Streets
- Innovative Stormwater Management
- Utility Undergrounding
- Roadway Reconstruction

Proposed Funding Source:
- Tax Increment Financing (TIF)

Status: In Design

Project Manager: Pinal Gandhi-Savdas

Micro Action Plan (MAP): Banner Lake

The Banner Lake Micro Action Plan (MAP) includes potential projects in Banner Lake neighborhood which includes bus shelter, crosswalks, traffic calming, intersection improvements, bike racks, and sidewalks.

The Banner Lake Club will engage the community to prioritize projects in the neighborhood. Staff will modify the Hobe Sound Community Redevelopment Plan to incorporate the Banner Lake MAP and allocate Tax Increment Finance (TIF) fund to assist in implementation.

Project Type:
- Community Outreach
- Master Planning

Funding Source:
- Staff Time
- Tax Increment Financing (TIF)

Status:
- Proposed

Project Manager: Pinal Gandhi-Savdas

1. Intersection Date Street/Lantana Ave.
2. Bus shelter location
3. Pedestrian priority/traffic calming area
4. Permanent Bike Rack
5. Intersection Citrus Way/Lantana Avenue
6. Sidewalk on Citrus

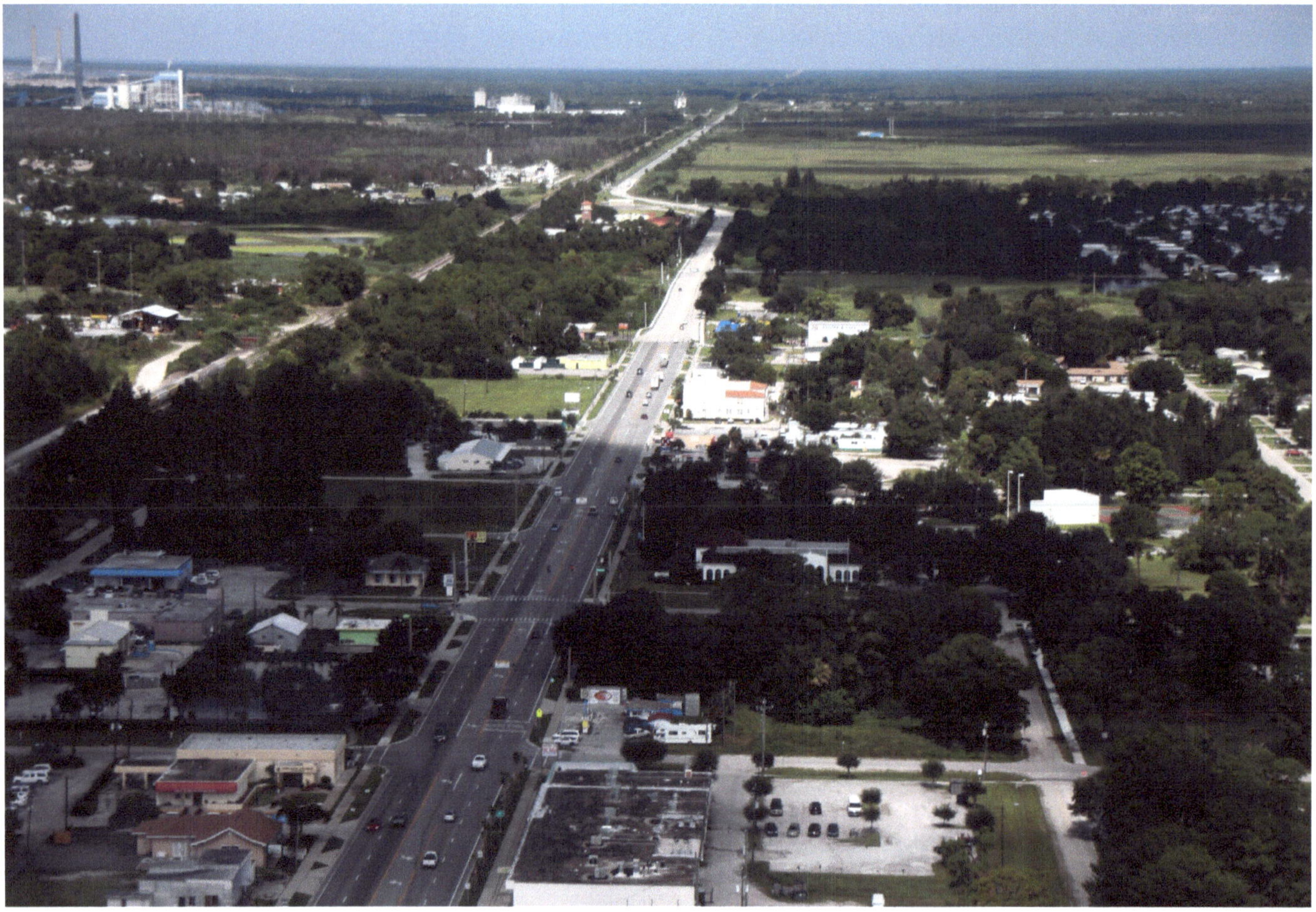

Area Summary

CRA Area: Indiantown

Plan Adoption: December 2002

Total Area: 5,083 Acres

Area Highlights:

- Largest rural community within Martin County.
- Strong transportation infrastructure that includes State Road 710, CSX Railway, the C-44 Canal, and Indiantown Airport.

Special Designations:

- Designated Florida Enterprise Zone

Indiantown

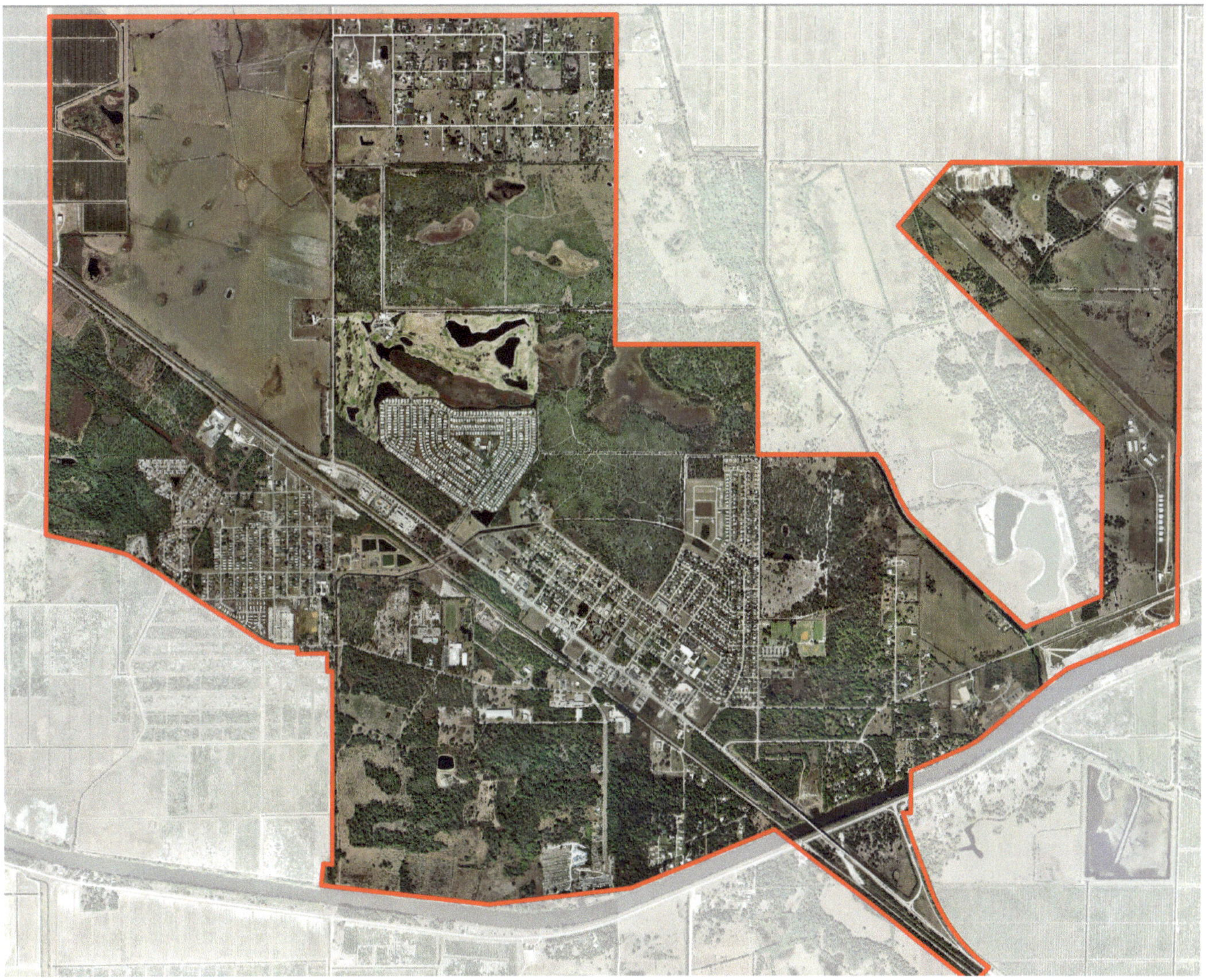

Village Square II

The Village Square II development is the second commercial development and first retail/office development in Indiantown in 20 years. This development includes a 1,745 sq. ft. Dunkin Donuts with a drive through and a detached 3,167 sq. ft. retail/office building. The development received final site plan approval in 2014. The development will break ground in early 2015, and should be open in the summer of 2015.

Village Square II is the located on Warfield Boulevard and is within the Indiantown Town Center Zoning Overlay District and is designated for Commercial General Use on the Future Land Use Map (FLUM) of the Comprehensive Growth Management Plan (CGMP).

Community Development Staff worked with the development team to fulfill the community vision for commercial development on Warfield Boulevard. Staff assisted in the site layout which maximizes the commercial building frontage on Warfield Boulevard. This collaboration allows for modular improvements to the surrounding streets, and encourages future infill development on this site.

The 2014 tax rolls generated by the Martin County Property Appraiser only reflect the development approval of this site. These records show a 161% percent increase in land value from the previous year the vertical improvements of over $1.5 million will be reflected in the 2015 taxable value, and will add to the tax base in Indiantown.

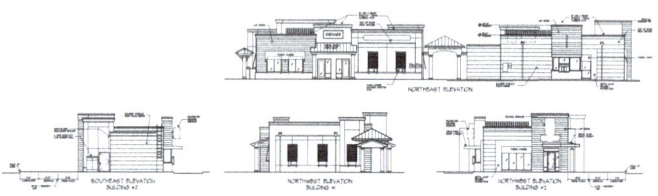

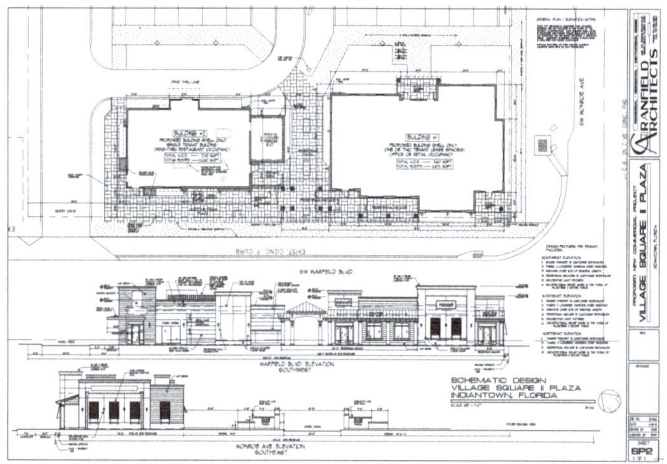

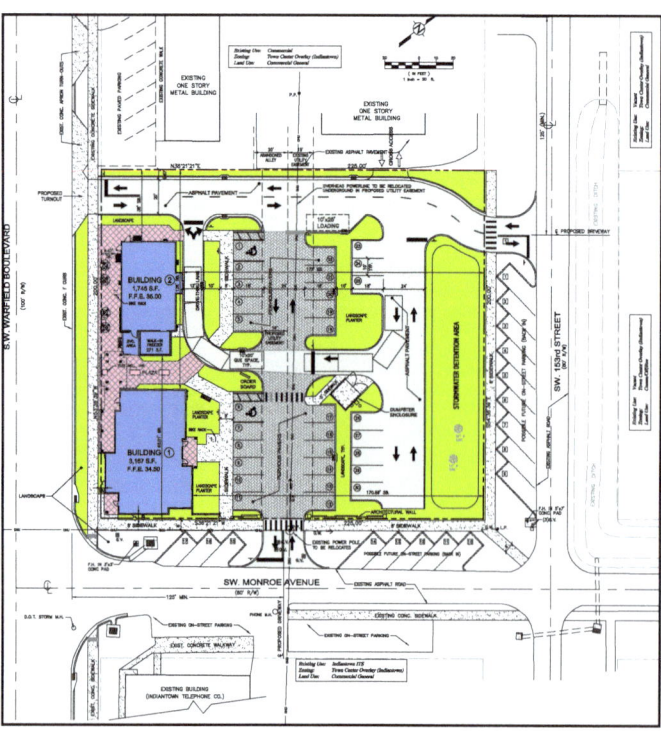

Project Type: Private Development
Funding Source:
- Staff Allocation
- Private Investment

Status: Approved Development Order
Project Manager: Edward W. Erfurt

Carter Park

Carter Park is a growing neighborhood in Indiantown. The new homes built in 2013 and 2014, provided new market comparable home sales within Indiantown. These sales were used by private sector developers who began construction and sales of new homes throughout Indiantown. This new construction is reflected in the growth of the tax base and TIF in Indiantown.

Carter Park has become a national and state model for public/private partnerships and community building. Carter Park received an Award of Merit by the Florida Chapter of the American Planning Association (APA). APA Florida celebrates the outstanding planning projects across the state that demonstrates innovation, transferability, quality, implementation, and comprehensiveness, at its annual conference.

Habitat for Humanity built and dedicated four additional affordable and green homes in Carter Park, and is preparing work for three additional homes. In addition to fulfilling the need for quality affordable housing, the Martin County Property Appraiser is reporting an increase in taxable value for these properties. The tax bills for the first two homes exceed the previous tax bill for the entire pre-development 12 acre site. As additional families move into this community, the tax revenue will continue to grow.

The Boys and Girls Club completed construction of the new 22,000 square foot Club which has been named the Bill and Barbara Whitman Indiantown Branch. The opening of the club included a visit and keynote speech from Jim Clark, the presidents and CEO of Boys & Girls Clubs of America. Mr. Clark noted how the Carter Park Club inspired the hard work of the Whitman's and how this type of partnership could be repeated within the national organization.

Project Type:
- Affordable Housing Development
- Innovative Stormwater Management
- Parks and Recreation

Funding Source:
- Staff Allocation
- Private Investment

Status:
- Complete
- Private Development Underway

Project Manager: Edward W. Erfurt

Area Summary

CRA Area: Jensen Beach

Plan Adoption: September 2002

Total Area: 67

Area Highlights:

- Waterfront community with an existing marina and commercial docks
- Gateway to Hutchinson Island
- FEC Rail crossing and access

Special Designations:

- Jensen Beach Community Redevelopment Area

Martin County Board of County Commissioners

Your County, Your Community

Jensen Beach

Indian River Drive

The Community Development Department is collaborating with the Martin County Engineering Department and private property owners to improve Indian River Drive at Jensen Beach Boulevard.

These improvements include improvements at this intersection will improve stormwater management and prevent flooding on private property, connect the last missing section of sidewalk on the east side of Indian River Drive in the CRA, provide additional on-street parking, landscaping, and street lighting.

A portion of the funding for this roadway improvement will be from the required improvements for the Sundance Marina Development. Community Development Staff are coordinating these required right of way improvements with the larger project, which will maximize the investment of Martin County and the adjacent property owners.

Project Type:
- Streetscape enhancements

Proposed Funding Source:
- TIF
- 707 Repaving Funds
- Private Investment

Status:
- In Design

Project Manager: Edward W. Erfurt

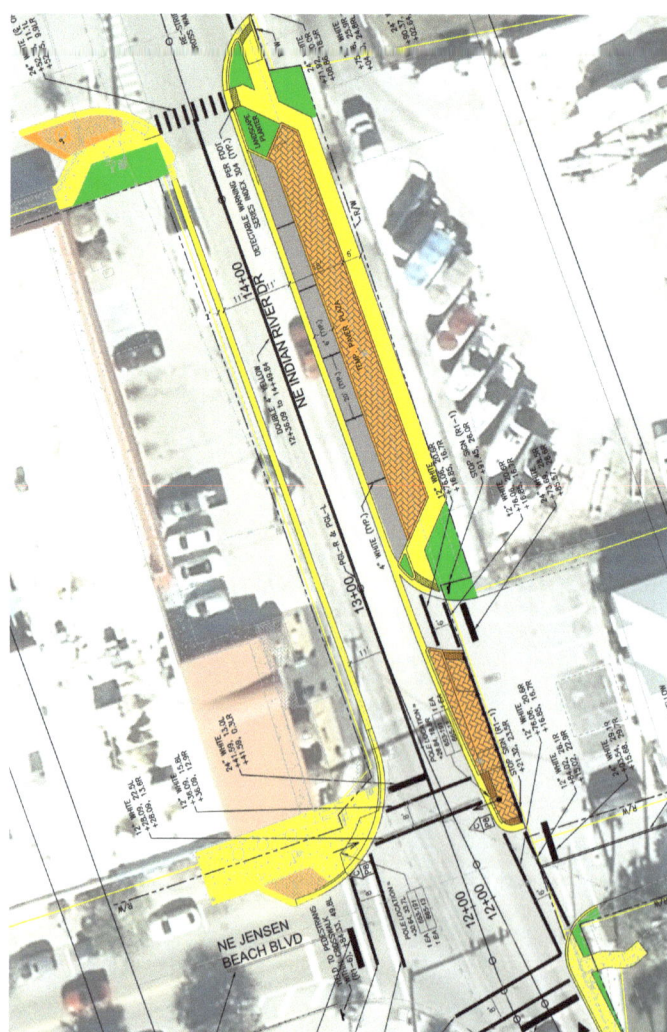

Jensen Beach Connector

Jensen Beach's unique history, small cottage businesses, dedicated residents, and its prime location on the Indian River, attract residents from the surrounding neighborhoods, many of which arrive through means of active transportation such as walking and biking. Community members reached out to Community Development staff to explore possible additional connections between Town of Ocean Breeze and downtown Jensen Beach.

Staff evaluated the existing conditions and identified four different alternatives as opportunities for additional safe active transportation connections: West End Boulevard, Maple and Melaleuca, Mid-Block Trail and Indian River Drive. After evaluating the 4 alternatives, Maple and Melaleuca was selected as priority by community members and the Jensen Beach Neighborhood Advisory Committee. The proximity of these streets, provided several opportunities to allow residents of the Town of Ocean Breeze to reach downtown Jensen.

Maple and Melaleuca Streets are low volume, low speed, streets that overlap along the Town of Ocean Breeze boundary. These streets were separated by sod and a six foot chain link fence. The project proposes an extension of the sidewalk from Jensen Beach Boulevard to Melaleuca Street and a fence opening to allow Town of Ocean Breeze neighborhood golf carts to connect with downtown Jensen Beach.

County staff is currently working in partnership with Town of Ocean Breeze Park representatives to coordinate the improvements to be made at each side of the proposed connection. The partnership would facilitate the introduction of additional improvements: sitting area, new fencing, landscape improvements and debris removal from a section of right of way to be transformed into open public space

Project Type:
- Interconnectivity
- Pedestrian accommodation

Funding Source:
- Tax Increment Financing (TIF)
- Private Investment

Status:
- In Design

Project Manager: Nancy Johnson

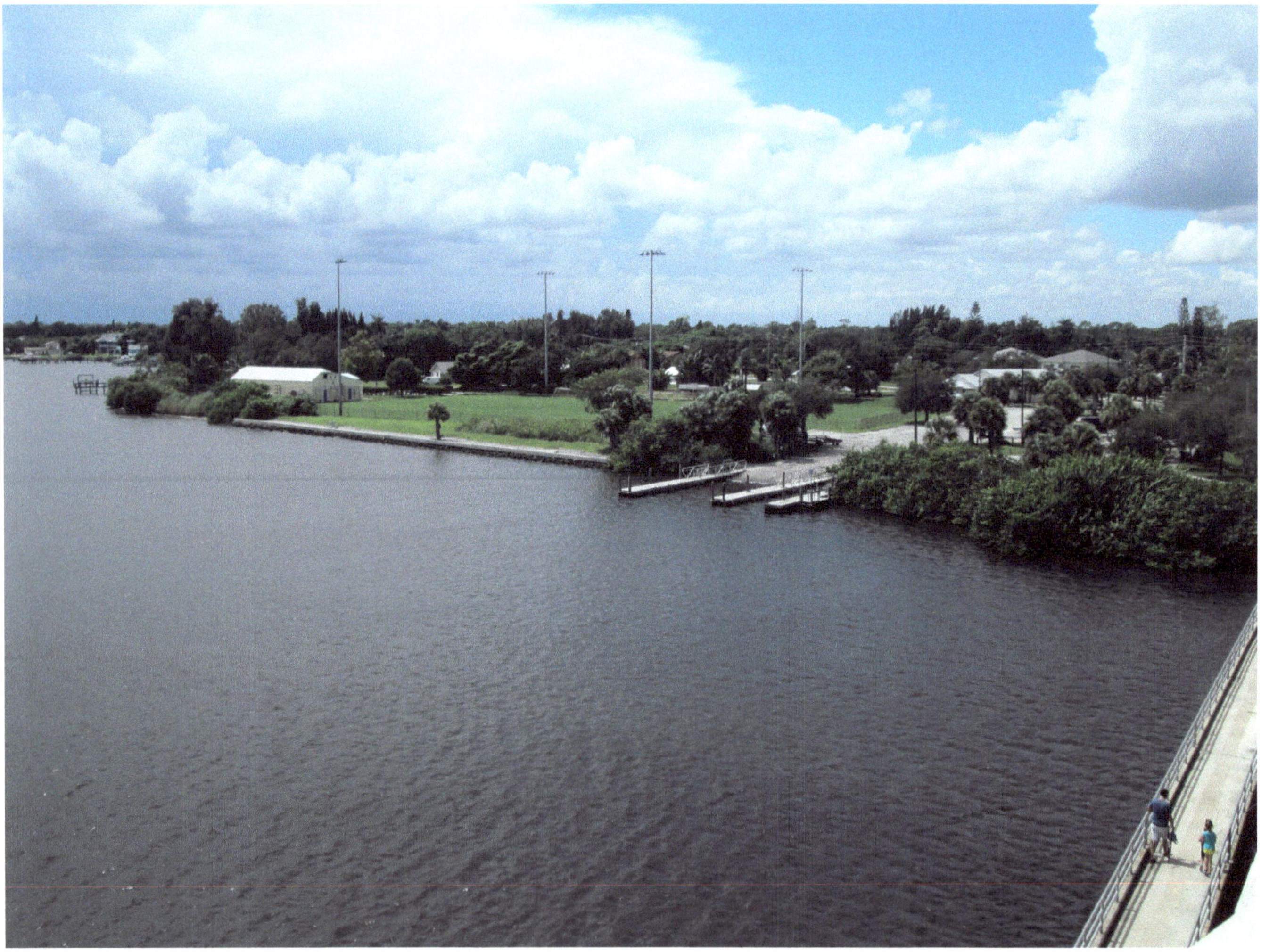

 # Area Summary

CRA Area: Old Palm City
Plan Adoption: April 2002
Total Area: 610 Acres
Area Highlights:
- Waterfront Community
- Home to Several Targeted Businesses

Special Designations:
- Old Palm City Community Redevelopment Area

Old Palm City

Mapp Road Town Center Design

Improvements for Mapp Road as outlined in the 2003 Old Palm City Redevelopment Plan included a desire for an old-fashioned Main Street, on-street parking, and a safe, well-connected corridor that allowed for various modes of transportation including walking and biking.

The CRA began in earnest in 2008 to make this project a reality. Engineering design drawings were prepared that included parallel parking, landscaped medians, and construction of a stormwater management system capable of handling future improvements.

In 2010, the design was updated utilizing more innovative strategies such as head out angled parking to replace parallel parking stalls, and rain gardens to better incorporate best stormwater management practices and improve environmental health. Center medians were removed as a cost saving measure and a modular design approach was introduced that did not require the entire roadway to be constructed all at once.

Through a series of public workshops led by staff in 2012, the community voiced their preference for a simpler design that would allow for construction of the entire corridor, rather than a modular approach.

Staff scheduled one-on-one meetings with business owners along the corridor. The CRA received 50% design plans in June 2014. The components of the design will be prioritized in keeping with the Community's desire. With $1.3 million available in TIF for construction, the CRA will phase the project that aligns with the available TIF dollars.

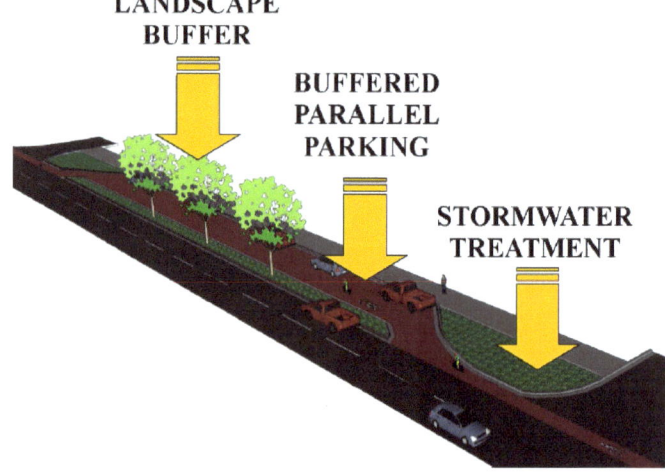

LANDSCAPE BUFFER

BUFFERED PARALLEL PARKING

STORMWATER TREATMENT

Project Type:
- Complete Streets
- Innovative Stormwater Management

Funding Source:
- Tax Increment Financing (TIF)

Status:
- In Design

Project Manager: Pinal Gandhi-Savdas

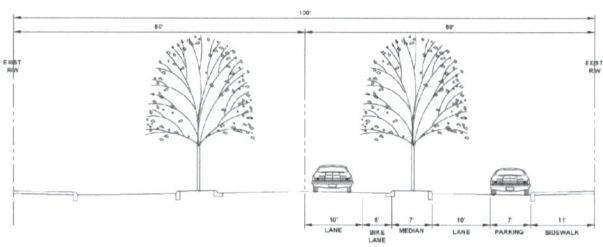

MAPP ROAD Blvd. Traditional Bike Lane Concept

Martin County Board of County Commissioners
Your County, Your Community

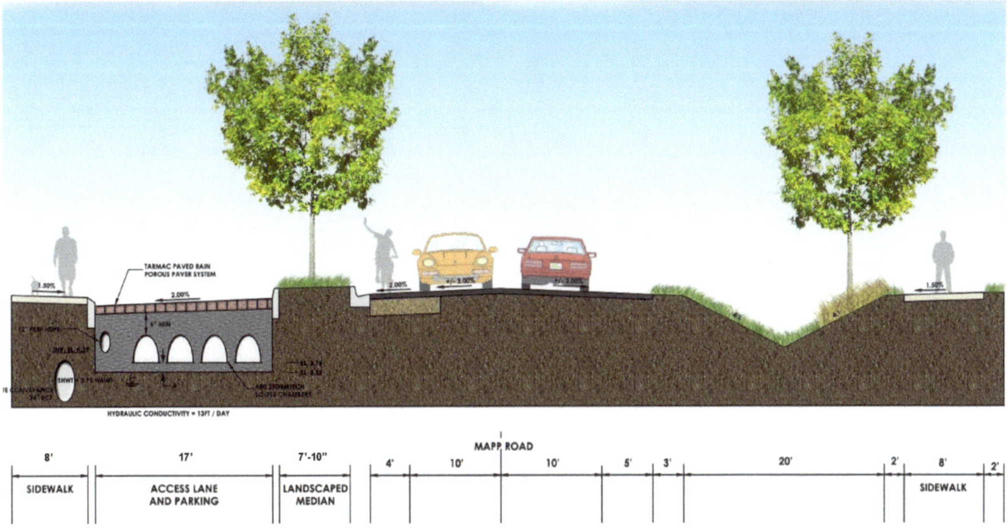

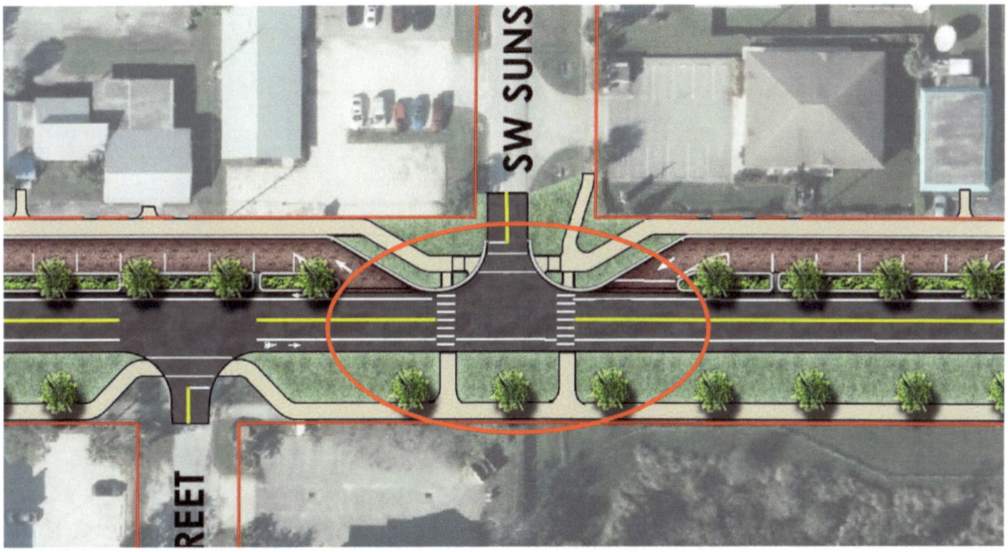

Above: *Innovative design allows for a modular approach which meet the immediate stormwater and pedestrian needs of Palm City while supporting future private redevelopment investment on Mapp Road.*

Martin County Community Redevelopment Agency

Redevelopment in Action

Demonstration Rain Garden – Mapp Road

As part of the Mapp Road Improvements project, a small demonstration rain garden was designed and installed on the east side of Mapp Road just north of SW 28th Street to receive runoff from hard surfaces such as sidewalk and roadway. This attractive, environmentally-friendly project allows water to infiltrate into the soil rather than becoming runoff. This helps to protect the quality of water downstream by preventing runoff from entering storm drains and helps reduce the chances for local flooding.

Rain gardens give stormwater a chance to slowly seep into the groundwater instead of rushing into storm drains all at once. In addition, rain gardens help to reduce the amount of sediment and other pollutants that runoff typically carries into drainage systems.

The rain garden was installed by Valley Crest Landscaping and was funded through Tax Increment Financing (TIF) funds.

Project Type:
- Innovative Stormwater Management

Funding Source:
- Staff Time
- Tax Increment Financing (TIF) $8,250

Status:
- Completed

Project Manager: Pinal Gandhi-Savdas

Charlie Leighton Park Accessible Floating Dock

The community vision for Charlie Leighton Park was outlined in 2003 with the adoption of the Old Palm City Redevelopment Plan. This vision included a focus on improved waterfront access, better identification signage, and incorporation of low-scale recreational uses such as canoe launches, passive park space, and walking trails. A more recent survey conducted in September of 2013 by the Martin County Community Development Department confirmed residents' ongoing desire for additional park amenities such as a floating dock, picnic facilities, and children's playground.

The waterfront access and shallow lagoon provides along the shores of Charlie Leighton Park provide a unique opportunity to support low impact human activities such as stand-up paddle boarding, rowing, and kayaking. The Charlie Leighton Park Accessible Floating Dock project proposes the installation of an ADA accessible floating dock to facilitate the safe launch of kayaks, paddleboards, rowing sculls and other low impact non-motorized recreational vessels.

The ADA accessible non-motorized boat launch will be the first of its kind in the County, allowing persons of all abilities to enjoy being on the water; the floating dock extension will accommodate users with oversized rowing shells. The project will provide opportunities for both active and passive recreational uses and enhance public access to the waterfront in keeping with the community vision. The proposed improvements will not negatively affect continued use of existing park facilities as all existing amenities will remain intact.

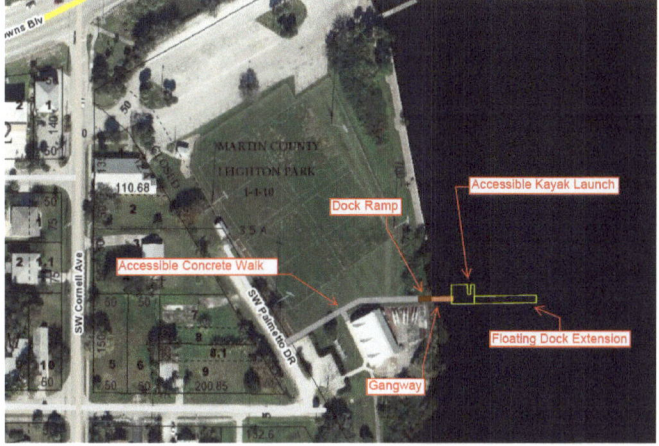

Project Type:
- Infrastructure

Funding Source:
- Tax Increment Finance (TIF)

Status:
- In Design

Project Manager: Nancy Johnson

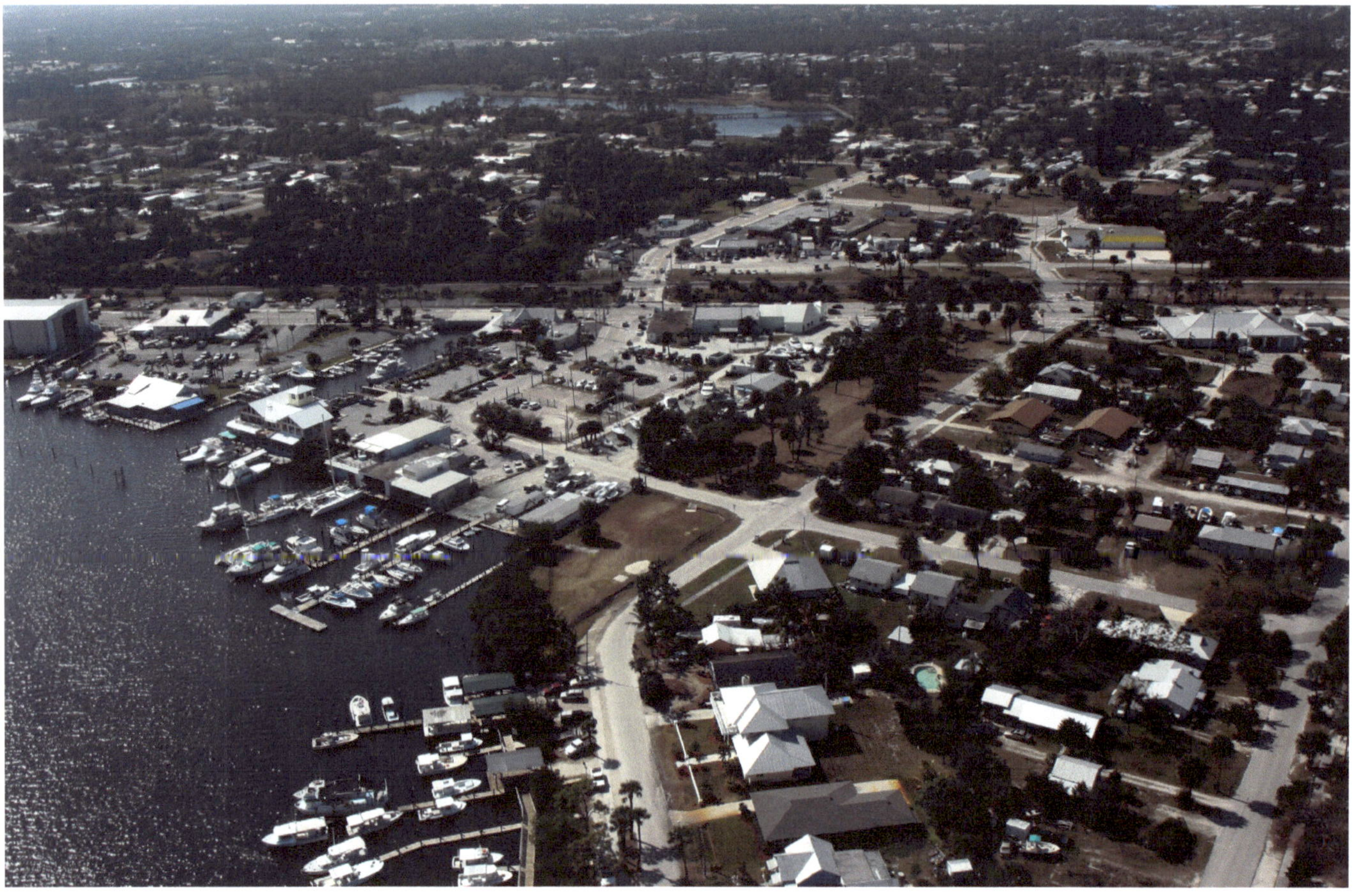

Area Summary

CRA Area: Port Salerno
Plan Adoption: May 2000
Total Area: 861 Acres
Area Highlights:
- Designated Florida waterfront community with residents and visitors enjoying the ever-increasing public waterfront access
- Economic base served largely by commercial and recreational fishing industry, in addition to boat manufacturing, repair and sales.

Special Designations:
- Waterfront Florida Community

Port Salerno

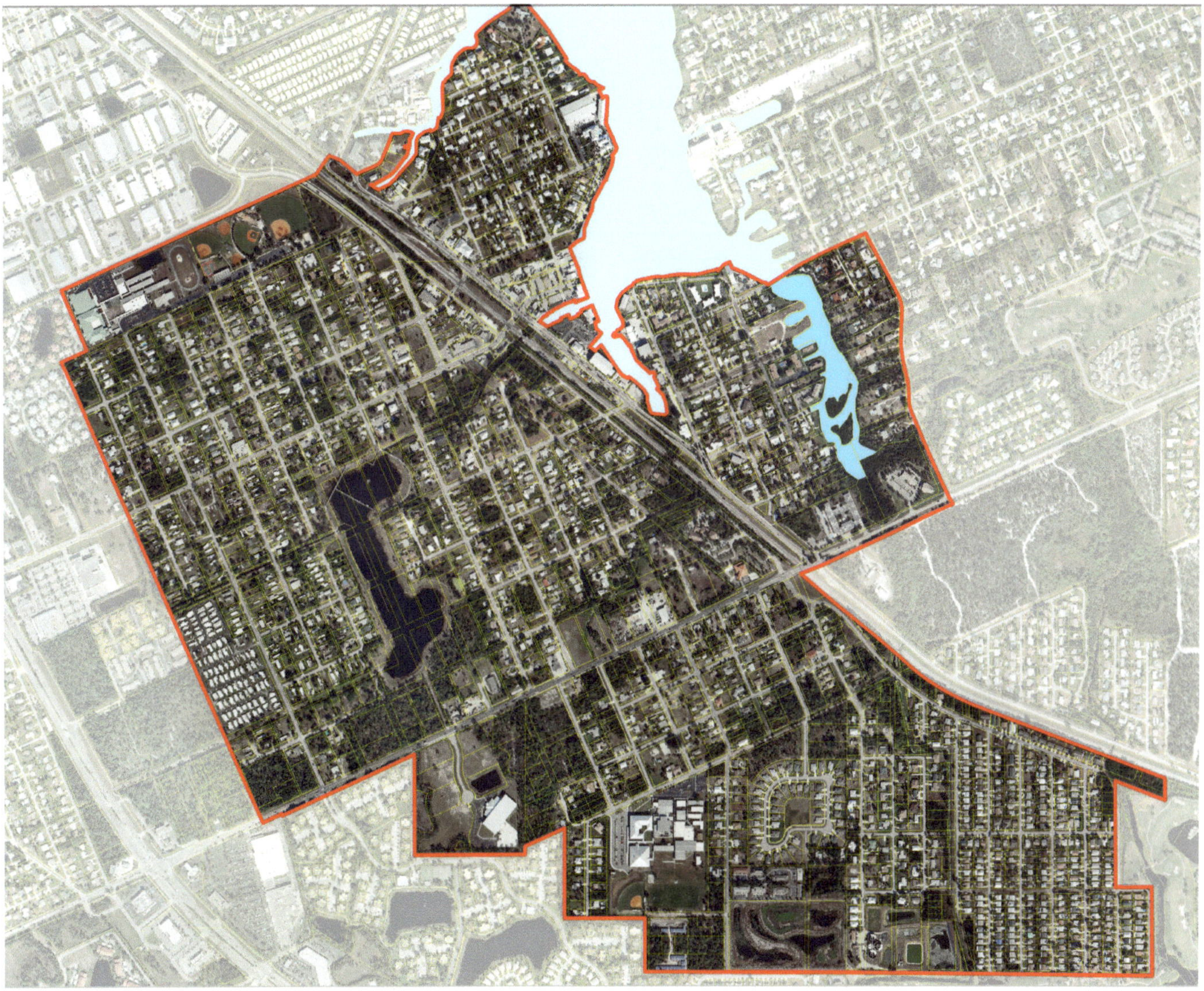

Commerce Avenue Demonstration Project

The success of several locally owned businesses in the Port Salerno Community Redevelopment Area has led to a greater need for public parking.

The Community Redevelopment Agency completed a preliminary analysis for the expansion of water of sewer in Port Salerno. The plan identified Commerce Avenue as a street that could be transformed to include on-street parking within the existing curb lines.

The Community Redevelopment Agency proposed a temporary demonstration project to add on-street parking to the west side of Commerce Avenue. This demonstration project was constructed at minimum cost, using temporary curbing and striping.

County Staff will monitor its success prior to making larger roadway improvements in the area.

Project Type:
- Complete Streets
- Public Parking

Funding Source:
- Tax Increment Financing (TIF)

Status:
- Complete

Project Manager: Erik Ferguson

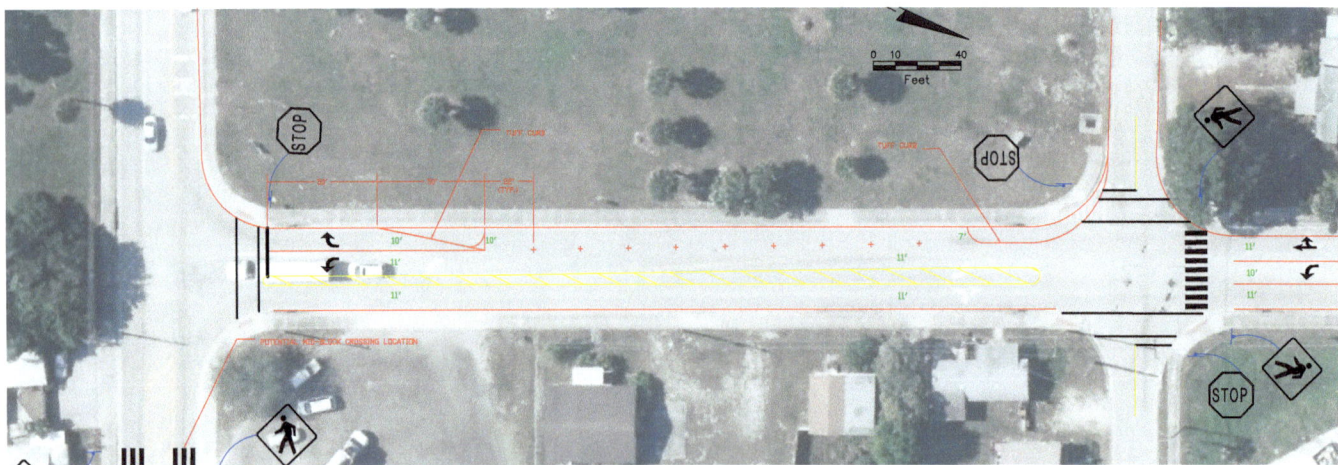

Manatee Creek MAP Phase I

The Manatee Creek Micro Action Plan (MAP) outlines potential projects throughout the Manatee Creek neighborhood which includes sidewalk connections, gateway signage, ditch cleanup, addition of landscaping, community park improvements to include perimeter fencing, and safety improvements such as street lighting and cleanup of brush and ditches.

At their August 20, 2013 BOCC meeting, the Board adopted the resolution modifying the Port Salerno Community Redevelopment Plan to Incorporate the Manatee Creek MAP and allocated funds from Port Salerno Tax Increment Finance (TIF) fund to assist in its implementation.

The Manatee Creek MAP Phase I project proposes the installation of landscape improvements and park fence along the Right of Way at SE Primrose Avenue, between SE Railway Avenue and SE Colee Avenue. The landscape improvements consist of Florida native and drought tolerant trees that will require low maintenance once established. These landscape improvements will not only obstruct the vehicular access outside of the travel lanes within the right of way but will also further the community vision to beautify the Manatee Creek neighborhood gateway.

Project Type:
- Gateway Enhancement

Funding Source:
- Tax Increment Financing (TIF)

Status:
- Design Complete
- Installation start first quarter FY15

Project Manager: Nancy Johnson

Salerno Road Sewer Enhancement

The Salerno Road Sewer Enhancement Project proposes a extension of the County's central sewer system on Salerno Road, from SE Commerce Avenue to Railway Avenue, and on Railway Avenue, from Salerno Road to 200 ft. north of Seaward St. which will enable existing businesses to utilize their full potential. The project will also introduce access management, on-street parking, pedestrian accommodations and low maintenance landscaping.

The benefits of the project go beyond the current scope, the lift station to be provided will enable additional sewer expansion into the residential neighborhoods to the west as funding becomes available in the future. The project includes a partnership with the Utilities Department.

Roadway improvements and utility design started on late June 2014 and is expected to be completed by mid 2015.

Project Type:
- Utilities
- Complete Streets

Funding Source:
- Tax Increment Financing (TIF)
- Utilities Department

Status:
- In Design

Project Manager: Nancy Johnson

Above: *Salerno Road today and the project area.*

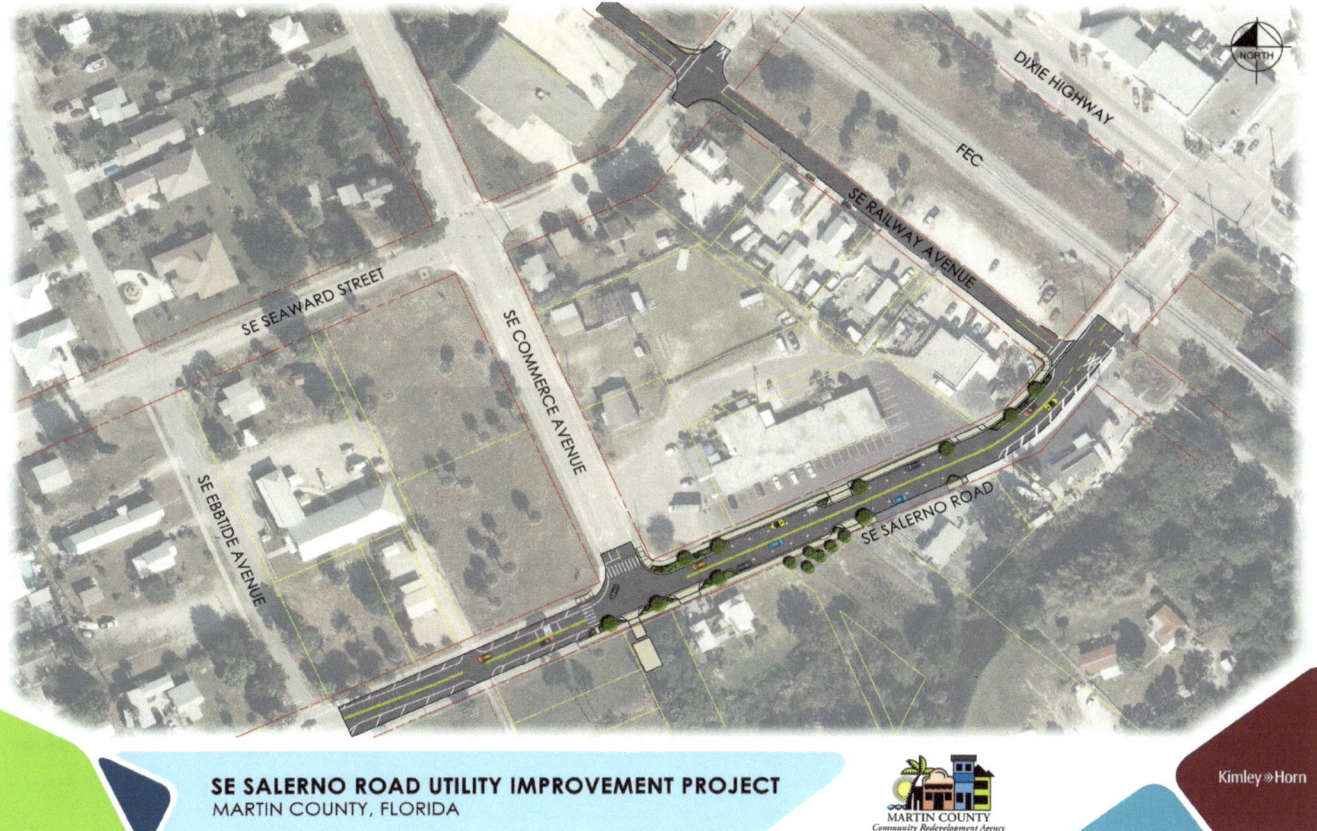

SE SALERNO ROAD UTILITY IMPROVEMENT PROJECT
MARTIN COUNTY, FLORIDA

Above: *Concept drawings for the improvements for Salerno Road. Staff and the project engineering are refining these ideas with each adjacent property owner to maximize the benefit of this project.*

Area Summary

CRA Area: Rio

Plan Adoption: April 2001

Total Area: 542 Acres

Area Highlights:

- Waterfront community with two existing marinas
- Wide economic base with a mix of commercial and industrial land uses and a private rail spur

Special Designations:

- Neighborhood Stabilization Program (NSP) Target Area

Martin County Board of County Commissioners
Your County, Your Community

Rio

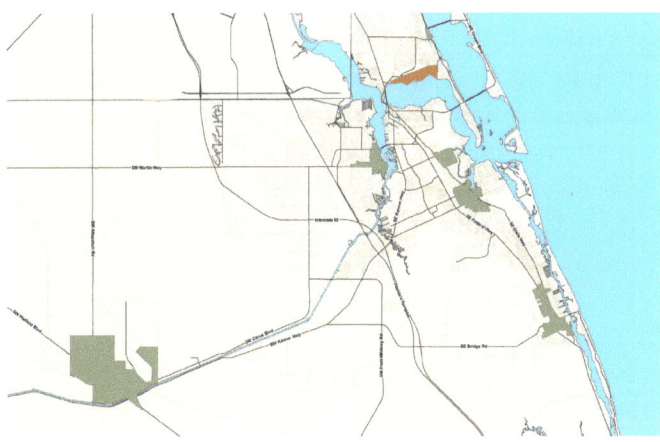

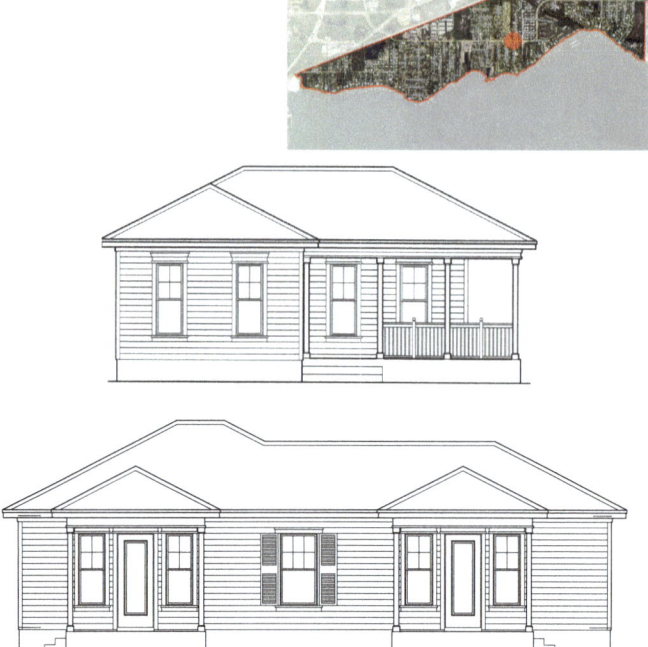

Rio Porches

Rio Porches is the former site of a deteriorated multiunit housing site within the Rio Town Center known as the Rainbow Cottages. In late 2011, the property was purchased via auction. Upon purchase, the new owners expressed an interest in partnering with the CRA to redevelop the site in a manner reflective of the community vision.

Through this partnership, the CRA assisted with demolition of the dilapidated structures, and successfully negotiated a donation of additional right-of-way along the CR-707 frontage. This facilitated the extension of the CR-707 Roadway Retrofit project to the east.

The 2014 tax rolls generated by the Martin County Property Appraiser only reflect the demolition of the previous structures and the development approval of this site. These records show a 105% percent increase in land value from the previous year and a 200% increase in value from the base year of the CRA.

The development currently under construction for two Live-Work Units, and six one bedroom cottages. the development already expanded the utility service south on Orange Avenue. Construction is scheduled to be completed in 2015.

Project Type:
- Mixed Use Redevelopment
- Infill Housing

Funding Source:
- Private Investment
- Tax Increment Financing (TIF) $75,000

Status:
- Public Utilities Expansion Complete
- Under Construction

Project Manager: Edward W. Erfurt

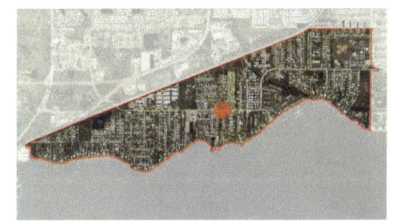

Rio Community Message Sign

The community requested an LED community message sign at Rio Civic Center in Rio. The request was made primarily due to the existing manual changeable pole sign at the Civic Center nearing the end of its useful life. The sign purpose is to serve the public health, safety and welfare of the community by informing citizens quickly in an event of an emergency and it would also provide a way to share information of upcoming community events and public service announcements.

The community wants the structure holding the LED sign to incorporate architectural feature to create Rio community identity.

A variance for the sign from the BOCC and modification to the Rio Community Redevelopment Plan to incorporate the community message sign and allocate $15,000 from Rio Tax Increment Finance (TIF) fund to assist in its implementation will be required prior to installation.

Project Type:
- Signage
- Community Identity

Funding Source:
- Tax Increment Financing (TIF) $15,000
- Rio Civic Club contribution $15,000

Status:
- Design completed

Project Manager: Pinal Gandhi-Savdas

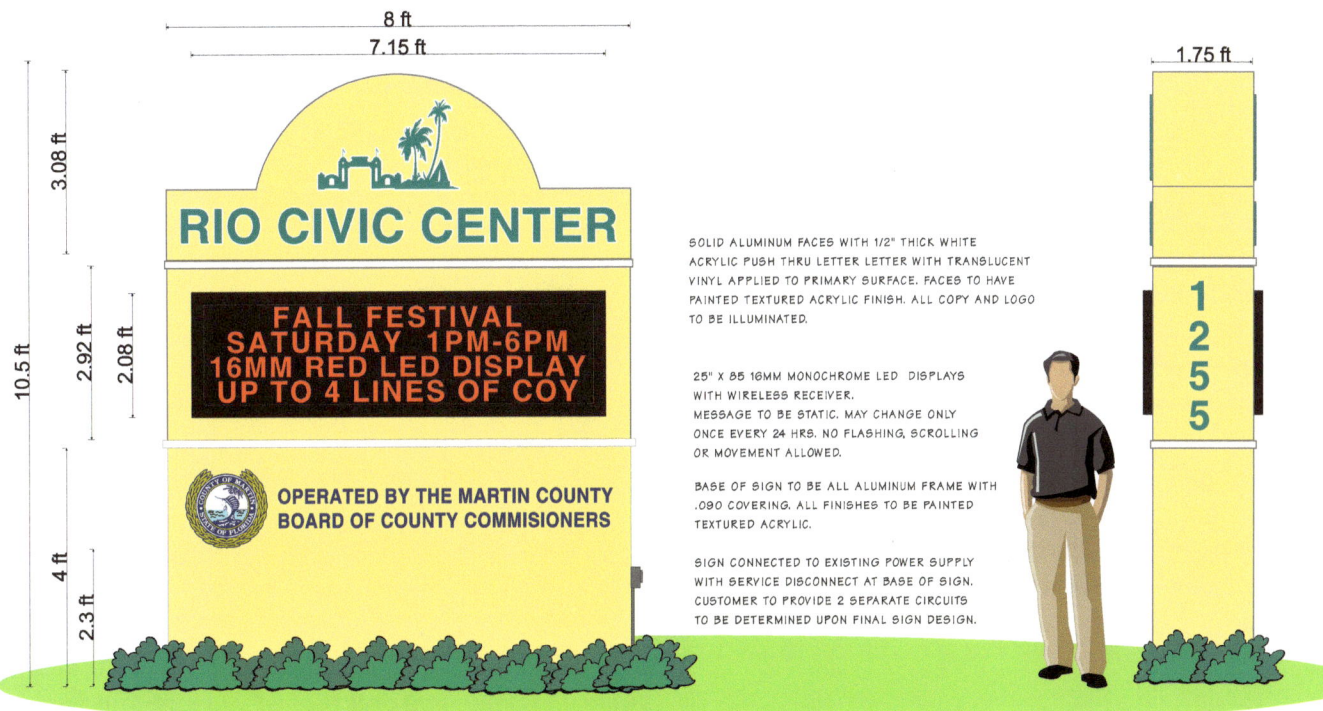

SOLID ALUMINUM FACES WITH 1/2" THICK WHITE ACRYLIC PUSH THRU LETTER LETTER WITH TRANSLUCENT VINYL APPLIED TO PRIMARY SURFACE. FACES TO HAVE PAINTED TEXTURED ACRYLIC FINISH. ALL COPY AND LOGO TO BE ILLUMINATED.

25" X 85 16MM MONOCHROME LED DISPLAYS WITH WIRELESS RECEIVER. MESSAGE TO BE STATIC. MAY CHANGE ONLY ONCE EVERY 24 HRS. NO FLASHING, SCROLLING OR MOVEMENT ALLOWED.

BASE OF SIGN TO BE ALL ALUMINUM FRAME WITH .090 COVERING. ALL FINISHES TO BE PAINTED TEXTURED ACRYLIC.

SIGN CONNECTED TO EXISTING POWER SUPPLY WITH SERVICE DISCONNECT AT BASE OF SIGN. CUSTOMER TO PROVIDE 2 SEPARATE CIRCUITS TO BE DETERMINED UPON FINAL SIGN DESIGN.

Western Rio Streetscape

The Western Rio Streetscape project is a partnership between the CRA and the Martin County Engineering Department on maximizing the benefits of a repaving project. Using the CRA vision as a framework and the recent town center improvements as a model, staff was able to develop an innovative street section that includes a safe pedestrian walkway, improved stormwater management, on-street parking and landscaping located along the south side of NE Dixie Highway between NE Sumner Avenue and NE Banyan Tree Drive.

This project resulted in slower speeds, an over-all reduction in impervious area (asphalt), and fixed several drainage issues in this area. All of this work was completed in the existing right of way and did not require any right of way acquisition. Property owners adjacent to these improvements have made noticeable improvements to their properties.

The landscape palette was developed under the direction of county staff and with the input from the Rio Neighborhood Advisory Committee. The resulting selections are native and complementary to the town center landscaping, and drought tolerant which reduces long term maintenance.

Above: *Existing conditions on 707 Dixie Highway.*

Project Type:
- Complete Street
- Stormwater
- Public Parking

Funding Source:
- Staff Time
- Tax Increment Financing (TIF)
- Martin County Engineering Resurfacing

Status:
- Under Construction

Project Manager: Pinal Gandhi-Savdas and Erik Ferguson

Above: *Milling of 707 Dixie highway, removing over 18 inches of asphalt laid over the last 50 years. The first step in improving the stormwater of the roadway.*

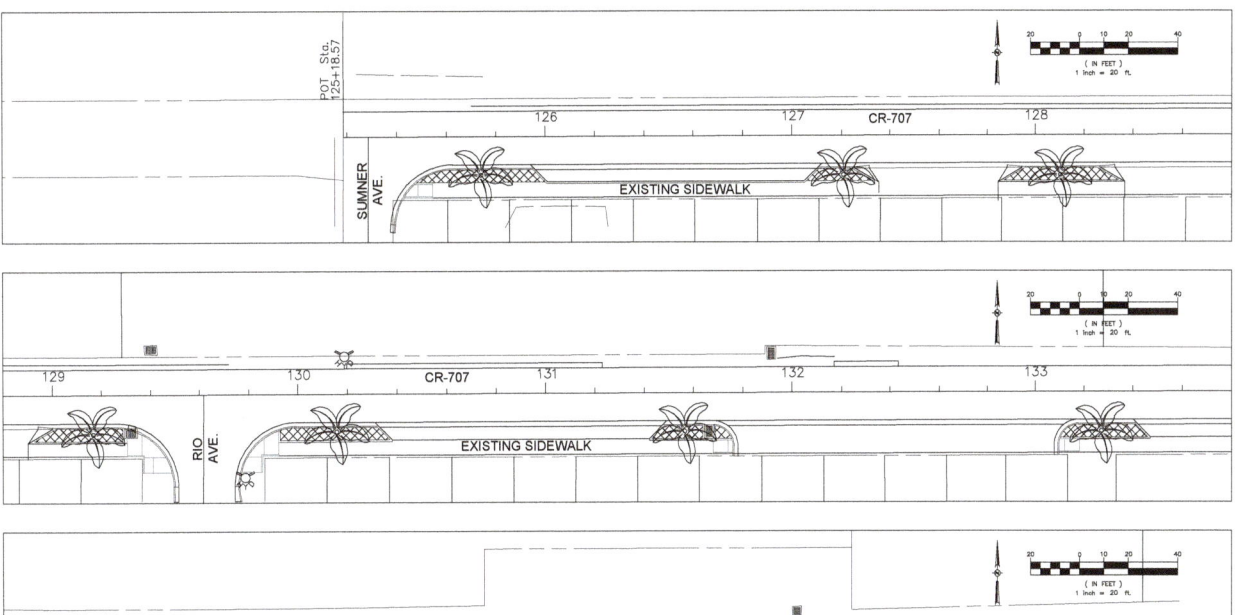

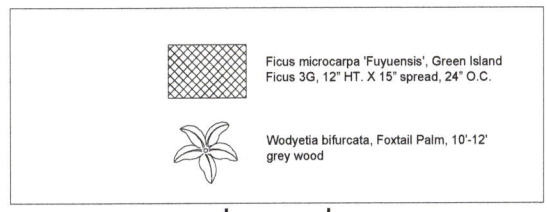

Ficus microcarpa 'Fuyuensis', Green Island
Ficus 3G, 12" HT. X 15" spread, 24" O.C.

Wodyetia bifurcata, Foxtail Palm, 10'-12'
grey wood

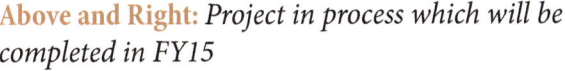

Above and Right: *Project in process which will be completed in FY15*

MARTIN COUNTY
Community Redevelopment Agency

MARTIN COUNTY BOARD OF COUNTY COMMISSIONERS

District 1	Doug Smith
District 2	Ed Fielding, Chair
District 3	Ann Scott, Vice Chair
District 4	Sarah Heard
District 5	John Haddox

MARTIN COUNTY COMMUNITY REDEVELOPMENT AGENCY

District 1	Doug Smith
District 2	Ed Fielding, Chair
District 3	Ann Scott, Vice Chair
District 4	Sarah Heard
District 5	John Haddox

COMMUNITY DEVELOPMENT STAFF

Kev Freeman, Director
Edward Erfurt, Urban Designer
Nancy Johnson, Community Development Specialist
Pinal Gandhi-Savdas, Community Development Specialist
Erik Ferguson, PE, Project Engineer

Dynamic   Innovative   Sustainable